OBJECT-ORIENTED JAVASCRIPT

THE PRINCIPLES OF
OBJECT-ORIENTED
JAVASCRIPT

by Nicholas C. Zakas

**no starch
press**

San Francisco

Printed in USA
First printing

18 17 16 15 14   1 2 3 4 5 6 7 8 9

Text stock is SFI certified

ISBN-10: 1-59327-540-4
ISBN-13: 978-1-59327-540-2

Publisher: William Pollock
Production Editor: Serena Yang
Cover Illustration: Charlie Wylie
Interior Design: Octopod Studios
Developmental Editor: Jennifer Griffith-Delgado
Technical Reviewer: Angus Croll
Copyeditor: Rachel Monaghan
Compositor: Serena Yang
Proofreader: Elaine Merrill
Indexer: Nancy Guenther

For information on distribution, translations, or bulk sales, please contact No Starch Press, Inc. directly:

No Starch Press, Inc.
245 8th Street, San Francisco, CA 94103
phone: 415.863.9900; fax: 415.863.9950; info@nostarch.com; www.nostarch.com

Library of Congress Cataloging-in-Publication Data

```
Zakas, Nicholas C.
  The principles of object-oriented JavaScript / by Nicholas C. Zakas.
      pages cm
  Includes index.
  ISBN-13: 978-1-59327-540-2 (paperback)
  ISBN-10: 1-59327-540-4 (paperback)
 1.  JavaScript (Computer program language) 2.  Object-oriented programming languages.  I. Title.
  QA76.73.J39Z357 2014
  005.1'17--dc23
                              2013048973
```

About the Author

Nicholas C. Zakas is a software engineer at Box and is known for writing on and speaking about the latest in JavaScript best practices. He honed his experience during his five years at Yahoo!, where he was principal frontend engineer for the Yahoo! home page. He is the author of several books, including *Maintainable JavaScript* (O'Reilly Media, 2012) and *Professional JavaScript for Web Developers* (Wrox, 2012).

About the Technical Reviewer

Originally from the UK, Angus Croll is now part of Twitter's web framework team in San Francisco and is the co-author and principal maintainer of Twitter's open source Flight framework. He's obsessed with JavaScript and literature in equal measure and is a passionate advocate for the greater involvement of artists and creative thinkers in software development. Angus is a frequent speaker at conferences worldwide and is currently working on two books for No Starch Press. He can be reached on Twitter at @angustweets.

BRIEF CONTENTS

CONTENTS IN DETAIL

3
UNDERSTANDING OBJECTS   31

4
CONSTRUCTORS AND PROTOTYPES   49

5
INHERITANCE   65

6
OBJECT PATTERNS   79

INDEX   93

FOREWORD

The name Nicholas Zakas is synonymous with
JavaScript development itself. I could ramble on
for pages with his professional accolades, but I am
not going to do that. Nicholas is well-known as a
highly skilled JavaScript developer and author, and
he needs no introduction. However, I would like to
offer some personal thoughts before praising the
contents of this book.

My relationship with Nicholas comes from years of studying his books,
reading his blog posts, watching him speak, and monitoring his Twitter
updates as a JavaScript pupil. We first met in person when I asked him
to speak at a jQuery conference several years ago. He treated the jQuery
community to a high-quality talk, and since then, we have spoken publicly
and privately over the Internet. In that time, I have come to admire him
as more than just a leader and developer in the JavaScript community.
His words are always gracious and thoughtful, his demeanor always kind.

His intent as a developer, speaker, and author is always to help, to educate, and to improve. When he speaks, you should listen, not just because he is a JavaScript expert, but because his character rises above his professional status.

This book's title and introduction make Nicholas's intentions clear: he has written it to help class-minded (that is, C++ or Java) programmers transition to a language without classes. In the book, he explains how encapsulation, aggregation, inheritance, and polymorphism can be accomplished when writing JavaScript. This is the ideal text to bring a knowledgeable programmer into the fold of object-oriented JavaScript development. If you are reading this book as a developer from another language, you are about to be treated to a concise and skillfully worded JavaScript book.

However, this book also stands to serve programmers coming from within the JavaScript fold. Many JavaScript developers have only an ECMAScript 3 (ES3) understanding of objects, and they are in need of a proper introduction to ECMAScript 5 (ES5) object features. This book can serve as that introduction, bridging a knowledge gap between ES3 objects and ES5 objects.

Now, you might be thinking, "Big deal. Several books have included chapters or notes on the additions to JavaScript found in ES5." Well, that is true. However, I believe this to be the only book written to date that focuses on the nature of objects by giving ES5 objects first-class citizenship in the entire narrative. This book brings a cohesive introduction to not only ES5 objects, but also the bits of ES3 that you need to grok while learning many of the new additions found in ES5.

As an author myself, I strongly believe this is the one book, given its focus on object-oriented principles and ES5 object updates, that needed to be written as we await ES6 updates to scripting environments.

Cody Lindley (*www.codylindley.com*)
Author of *JavaScript Enlightenment, DOM Enlightenment,*
    and *jQuery Enlightenment*
Boise, Idaho
December 16, 2013

ACKNOWLEDGMENTS

I'd like to thank Kate Matsudaira for convincing me that self-publishing an ebook was the best way to get this information out. Without her advice, I'd probably still be trying to figure out what I should do with the information contained in this book.

Thanks to Rob Friesel for once again providing excellent feedback on an early copy of this book, and Cody Lindley for his suggestions. Additional thanks to Angus Croll for his technical review of the finished version—his nitpicking made this book much better.

Thanks as well to Bill Pollock, whom I met at a conference and who started the ball rolling on publishing this book.

INTRODUCTION

Most developers associate object-oriented programming with languages that are typically taught in school, like C++ and Java, which base object-oriented programming around classes. Before you can do anything in these languages, you need to create a class, even if you're just writing a simple command-line program. Common design patterns in the industry reinforce class-based concepts as well. But JavaScript doesn't use classes, and this is part of the reason people get confused when they try learning it after C++ or Java.

Object-oriented languages have several characteristics:

Encapsulation   Data can be grouped together with functionality that operates on that data. This, quite simply, is the definition of an object.

Aggregation   One object can reference another object.

Inheritance   A newly created object has the same characteristics as another object without explicitly duplicating its functionality.

Polymorphism   One interface may be implemented by multiple objects.

JavaScript has all these characteristics, though because the language has no concept of classes, some aren't implemented in quite the way you might expect. At first glance, a JavaScript program might even look like a procedural program you would write in C. If you can write a function and pass it some variables, you have a working script that seemingly has no objects. A closer look at the language, however, reveals the existence of objects through the use of dot notation.

Many object-oriented languages use dot notation to access properties and methods on objects, and JavaScript is syntactically the same. But in JavaScript, you never need to write a class definition, import a package, or include a header file. You just start coding with the data types that you want, and you can group those together in any number of ways. You could certainly write JavaScript in a procedural way, but its true power emerges when you take advantage of its object-oriented nature. That's what this book is about.

Make no mistake: A lot of the concepts you may have learned in more traditional object-oriented programming languages don't necessarily apply to JavaScript. While that often confuses beginners, as you read, you'll quickly find that JavaScript's weakly typed nature allows you to write less code to accomplish the same tasks as other languages. You can just start coding without planning the classes that you need ahead of time. Need an object with specific fields? Just create an ad hoc object wherever you want. Did you forget to add a method to that object? No problem—just add it later.

Inside these pages, you'll learn the unique way that JavaScript approaches object-oriented programming. Leave behind the notions of classes and class-based inheritance and learn about prototype-based inheritance and constructor functions that behave similarly. You'll learn how to create objects, define your own types, use inheritance, and otherwise manipulate objects to get the most out of them. In short, you'll learn everything you need to know to understand and write JavaScript professionally. Enjoy!

Who This Book Is For

This book is intended as a guide for those who already understand object-oriented programming but want to know exactly how the concept works in JavaScript. Familiarity with Java, C#, or object-oriented programming in other languages is a strong indicator that this book is for you. In particular, this book is aimed at three groups of readers:

- Developers who are familiar with object-oriented programming concepts and want to apply them to JavaScript
- Web application and Node.js developers trying to structure their code more effectively
- Novice JavaScript developers trying to gain a deeper understanding of the language

This book is not for beginners who have never written JavaScript. You will need a good understanding of how to write and execute JavaScript code to follow along.

Overview

Chapter 1: Primitive and Reference Types introduces the two different value types in JavaScript: primitive and reference. You'll learn what distinguishes them from each other and how understanding their differences is important to an overall understanding of JavaScript.

Chapter 2: Functions explains the ins and outs of functions in JavaScript. First-class functions are what makes JavaScript such an interesting language.

Chapter 3: Understanding Objects details the makeup of objects in JavaScript. JavaScript objects behave differently than objects in other languages, so a deep understanding of how objects work is vital to mastering the language.

Chapter 4: Constructors and Prototypes expands on the previous discussion of functions by looking more specifically at constructors. All constructors are functions, but they are used a little bit differently. This chapter explores the differences while also talking about creating your own custom types.

Chapter 5: Inheritance explains how inheritance is accomplished in JavaScript. Though there are no classes in JavaScript, that doesn't mean inheritance isn't possible. In this chapter, you'll learn about prototypal inheritance and how it differs from class-based inheritance.

Chapter 6: Object Patterns walks through common object patterns. There are many different ways to build and compose objects in JavaScript, and this chapter introduces you to the most popular patterns for doing so.

Help and Support

If you have questions, comments, or other feedback about this book, please visit the mailing list at *http://groups.google.com/group/zakasbooks*.

1

PRIMITIVE AND REFERENCE TYPES

Most developers learn object-oriented programming by working with class-based languages such as Java or C#. When these developers start learning JavaScript, they get disoriented because JavaScript has no formal support for classes. Instead of defining classes from the beginning, with JavaScript you can just write code and create data structures as you need them. Because it lacks classes, JavaScript also lacks class groupings such as packages. Whereas in languages like Java, package and class names define both the types of objects you use and the layout of files and folders in your project, programming in JavaScript is like starting with a blank slate: You can organize things any way you want. Some developers choose to mimic structures from other languages, while others take advantage of Java-Script's flexibility to come up with something completely new. To the uninitiated, this freedom of choice can be overwhelming, but once you get used to it, you'll find JavaScript to be an incredibly flexible language that can adapt to your preferences quite easily.

To ease the transition from traditional object-oriented languages, JavaScript makes objects the central part of the language. Almost all data in JavaScript is either an object or accessed through objects. In fact, even functions (which languages traditionally make you jump through hoops to get references to) are represented as objects in JavaScript, which makes them *first-class functions*.

Working with and understanding objects is key to understanding Java-Script as a whole. You can create objects at any time and add or remove properties from them whenever you want. In addition, JavaScript objects are extremely flexible and have capabilities that create unique and inter-esting patterns that are simply not possible in other languages.

This chapter focuses on how to identify and work with the two pri-mary JavaScript data types: primitive types and reference types. Though both are accessed through objects, they behave in different ways that are important to understand.

What Are Types?

Although JavaScript has no concept of classes, it still uses two kinds of *types*: primitive and reference. *Primitive types* are stored as simple data types. *Reference types* are stored as objects, which are really just references to locations in memory.

The tricky thing is that JavaScript lets you treat primitive types like reference types in order to make the language more consistent for the developer.

While other programming languages distinguish between primitive and reference types by storing primitives on the stack and references in the heap, JavaScript does away with this concept completely: It tracks variables for a particular scope with a *variable object*. Primitive values are stored directly on the variable object, while reference values are placed as a pointer in the variable object, which serves as a reference to a location in memory where the object is stored. However, as you'll see later in this chapter, primitive values and reference values behave quite differently although they may initially seem the same.

Of course, there are other differences between primitive and refer-ence types.

Primitive Types

Primitive types represent simple pieces of data that are stored as is, such as true and 25. There are five primitive types in JavaScript:

Boolean	true or false
Number	Any integer or floating-point numeric value
String	A character or sequence of characters delimited by either single or double quotes (JavaScript has no separate character type)
Null	A primitive type that has only one value, null
Undefined	A primitive type that has only one value, undefined (undefined is the value assigned to a variable that is not initialized)

The first three types (Boolean, number, and string) behave in similar ways, while the last two (null and undefined) work a bit differently, as will be discussed throughout this chapter. All primitive types have literal representations of their values. *Literals* represent values that aren't stored in a variable, such as a hardcoded name or price. Here are some examples of each type using its literal form:

```
// strings
var name = "Nicholas";
var selection = "a";

// numbers
var count = 25;
var cost = 1.51;

// boolean
var found = true;

// null
var object = null;

// undefined
var flag = undefined;
var ref;     // assigned undefined automatically
```

In JavaScript, as in many other languages, a variable holding a primitive directly contains the primitive value (rather than a pointer to an object). When you assign a primitive value to a variable, the value is copied into that variable. This means that if you set one variable equal to another, each variable gets its own copy of the data. For example:

```
var color1 = "red";
var color2 = color1;
```

Here, color1 is assigned the value of "red". The variable color2 is then assigned the value color1, which stores "red" in color2. Even though color1 and color2 contain the same value, they are completely separate from each other, and you can change the value in color1 without affecting color2 and vice versa. That's because there are two different storage locations, one for each variable. Figure 1-1 illustrates the variable object for this snippet of code.

Variable Object	
color1	"red"
color2	"red"

Figure 1-1: Variable object

Because each variable containing a primitive value uses its own storage space, changes to one variable are not reflected on the other. For example:

```
var color1 = "red";
var color2 = color1;

console.log(color1);    // "red"
console.log(color2);    // "red"

color1 = "blue";

console.log(color1);    // "blue"
console.log(color2);    // "red"
```

In this code, color1 is changed to "blue" and color2 retains its original value of "red".

Identifying Primitive Types

The best way to identify primitive types is with the typeof operator, which works on any variable and returns a string indicating the type of data. The typeof operator works well with strings, numbers, Booleans, and undefined. The following shows the output when using typeof on different primitive values:

```
console.log(typeof "Nicholas");    // "string"
console.log(typeof 10);            // "number"
console.log(typeof 5.1);           // "number"
console.log(typeof true);          // "boolean"
console.log(typeof undefined);     // "undefined"
```

As you might expect, typeof returns "string" when the value is a string; "number" when the value is a number (regardless of integer or floating-point values); "boolean" when the value is a Boolean; and "undefined" when the value is undefined.

The tricky part involves null.

You wouldn't be the first developer to be confused by the result of this line of code:

```
console.log(typeof null);          // "object"
```

When you run typeof null, the result is "object". But why an object when the type is null? (In fact, this has been acknowledged as an error by TC39, the committee that designs and maintains JavaScript. You could reason that null is an empty object pointer, making "object" a logical return value, but that's still confusing.)

The best way to determine if a value is null is to compare it against null directly, like this:

```
console.log(value === null);          // true or false
```

COMPARING WITHOUT COERCION

Notice that this code uses the triple equals operator (===) instead of the double equals operator. The reason is that triple equals does the comparison without coercing the variable to another type. To understand why this is important, consider the following:

```
console.log("5" == 5);          // true
console.log("5" === 5);          // false

console.log(undefined == null);          // true
console.log(undefined === null);          // false
```

When you use the double equals, the string "5" and the number 5 are considered equal because the double equals converts the string into a number before it makes the comparison. The triple equals operator doesn't consider these values equal because they are two different types. Likewise, when you compare undefined and null, the double equals says that they are equivalent, while the triple equals says they are not. When you're trying to identify null, use triple equals so that you can correctly identify the type.

Primitive Methods

Despite the fact that they're primitive types, strings, numbers, and Booleans actually have methods. (The null and undefined types have no methods.) Strings, in particular, have numerous methods to help you work with them. For example:

```
var name = "Nicholas";
var lowercaseName = name.toLowerCase();     // convert to lowercase
var firstLetter = name.charAt(0);           // get first character
var middleOfName = name.substring(2, 5);    // get characters 2-4

var count = 10;
var fixedCount = count.toFixed(2);          // convert to "10.00"
var hexCount = count.toString(16);          // convert to "a"

var flag = true;
var stringFlag = flag.toString();           // convert to "true"
```

NOTE *Despite the fact that they have methods, primitive values themselves are not objects. JavaScript makes them look like objects to provide a consistent experience in the language, as you'll see later in this chapter.*

Reference Types

Reference types represent objects in JavaScript and are the closest things to classes that you will find in the language. Reference values are *instances* of reference types and are synonymous with objects (the rest of this chapter refers to reference values simply as *objects*). An object is an unordered list of *properties* consisting of a name (always a string) and a value. When the value of a property is a function, it is called a *method*. Functions themselves are actually reference values in JavaScript, so there's little difference between a property that contains an array and one that contains a function except that a function can be executed.

Of course, you must create objects before you can begin working with them.

Creating Objects

It sometimes helps to think of JavaScript objects as nothing more than hash tables, as shown in Figure 1-2.

There are a couple of ways to create, or *instantiate*, objects. The first is to use the new operator with a *constructor*. (A constructor is simply a function that uses new to create an object—any function can be

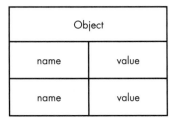

Figure 1-2: Structure of an object

a constructor.) By convention, constructors in JavaScript begin with a capital letter to distinguish them from nonconstructor functions. For example, this code instantiates a generic object and stores a reference to it in object:

```
var object = new Object();
```

Reference types do not store the object directly into the variable to which it is assigned, so the object variable in this example doesn't actually contain the object instance. Instead, it holds a pointer (or reference) to the location in memory where the object exists. This is the primary difference between objects and primitive values, as the primitive is stored directly in the variable.

When you assign an object to a variable, you're actually assigning a pointer. That means if you assign one variable to another, each variable gets a copy of the pointer, and both still reference the same object in memory. For example:

```
var object1 = new Object();
var object2 = object1;
```

This code first creates an object (with new) and stores a reference in object1. Next, object2 is assigned the value of object1. There is still only the one instance of the object that was created on the first line, but both variables now point to that object, as illustrated in Figure 1-3.

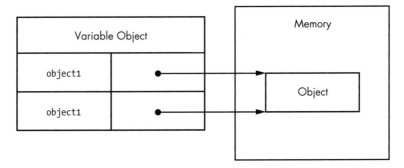

Figure 1-3: Two variables pointing to one object

Dereferencing Objects

JavaScript is a garbage-collected language, so you don't really need to worry about memory allocations when you use reference types. However, it's best to *dereference* objects that you no longer need so that the garbage collector can free up that memory. The best way to do this is to set the object variable to null.

```
var object1 = new Object();

// do something

object1 = null;      // dereference
```

Here, `object1` is created and used before finally being set to `null`. When there are no more references to an object in memory, the garbage collector can use that memory for something else. (Dereferencing objects is especially important in very large applications that use millions of objects.)

Adding or Removing Properties

Another interesting aspect of objects in JavaScript is that you can add and remove properties at any time. For example:

```
var object1 = new Object();
var object2 = object1;

object1.myCustomProperty = "Awesome!";
console.log(object2.myCustomProperty);      // "Awesome!"
```

Here, `myCustomProperty` is added to `object1` with a value of `"Awesome!"`. That property is also accessible on `object2` because both `object1` and `object2` point to the same object.

NOTE   *This example demonstrates one particularly unique aspect of JavaScript: You can modify objects whenever you want, even if you didn't define them in the first place. And there are ways to prevent such modifications, as you'll learn later in this book.*

In addition to generic object reference types, JavaScript has several other built-in types that are at your disposal.

Instantiating Built-in Types

You've seen how to create and interact with generic objects created with `new Object()`. The `Object` type is just one of a handful of built-in reference types that JavaScript provides. The other built-in types are more specialized in their intended usage and can be instantiated at any time.

The built-in types are:

Array   An ordered list of numerically indexed values

Date   A date and time

Error	A runtime error (there are also several more specific error subtypes)
Function	A function
Object	A generic object
RegExp	A regular expression

You can instantiate each built-in reference type using new, as shown here:

```
var items = new Array();
var now = new Date();
var error = new Error("Something bad happened.");
var func = new Function("console.log('Hi');");
var object = new Object();
var re = new RegExp("\\d+");
```

Literal Forms

Several built-in reference types have literal forms. A *literal* is syntax that allows you to define a reference value without explicitly creating an object, using the new operator and the object's constructor. (Earlier in this chapter, you saw examples of primitive literals including string literals, numeric literals, Boolean literals, the null literal, and the undefined literal.)

Object and Array Literals

To create an object with *object literal* syntax, you can define the properties of a new object inside braces. Properties are made up of an identifier or string, a colon, and a value, with multiple properties separated by commas. For example:

```
var book = {
    name: "The Principles of Object-Oriented JavaScript",
    year: 2014
};
```

You can also use string literals as property names, which is useful when you want a property name to have spaces or other special characters:

```
var book = {
    "name": "The Principles of Object-Oriented JavaScript",
    "year": 2014
};
```

This example is equivalent to the previous one despite the syntactic differences. Both examples are also logically equivalent to the following:

```
var book = new Object();
book.name = "The Principles of Object-Oriented JavaScript";
book.year = 2014;
```

The outcome of each of the previous three examples is the same: an object with two properties. The choice of pattern is up to you because the functionality is ultimately the same.

NOTE   *Using an object literal doesn't actually call* new Object()*. Instead, the JavaScript engine follows the same steps it does when using* new Object() *without actually calling the constructor. This is true for all reference literals.*

You can define an *array literal* in a similar way by enclosing any number of comma-separated values inside square brackets. For example:

```
var colors = [ "red", "blue", "green" ];
console.log(colors[0]);      // "red"
```

This code is equivalent to the following:

```
var colors = new Array("red", "blue", "green")
console.log(colors[0]);      // "red"
```

Function Literals

You almost always define functions using their literal form. In fact, using the Function constructor is typically discouraged given the challenges of maintaining, reading, and debugging a string of code rather than actual code, so you'll rarely see it in code.

Creating functions is much easier and less error prone when you use the literal form. For example:

```
function reflect(value) {
    return value;
}

// is the same as

var reflect = new Function("value", "return value;");
```

This code defines the reflect() function, which returns any value passed to it. Even in the case of this simple function, the literal form is easier to write and understand than the constructor form. Further, there is no good way to debug functions that are created in the constructor form: These functions aren't recognized by JavaScript debuggers and therefore act as a black box in your application.

Regular Expression Literals

JavaScript also has *regular expression literals* that allow you to define regular expressions without using the `RegExp` constructor. Regular expression literals look very similar to regular expressions in Perl: The pattern is contained between two slashes, and any additional options are single characters following the second slash. For example:

```
var numbers = /\d+/g;

// is the same as

var numbers = new RegExp("\\d+", "g");
```

The literal form of regular expressions in JavaScript is a bit easier to deal with than the constructor form because you don't need to worry about escaping characters within strings. When using the `RegExp` constructor, you pass the pattern in as a string, so you have to escape any backslashes. (That's why \d is used in the literal and \\d is used in the constructor.) Regular expression literals are preferred over the constructor form in JavaScript except when the regular expression is being constructed dynamically from one or more strings.

That said, with the exception of `Function`, there really isn't any right or wrong way to instantiate built-in types. Many developers prefer literals, while some prefer constructors. Choose whichever method you find more comfortable to use.

Property Access

Properties are name/value pairs that are stored on an object. Dot notation is the most common way to access properties in JavaScript (as in many object-oriented languages), but you can also access properties on JavaScript objects by using bracket notation with a string.

For example, you could write this code, which uses dot notation:

```
var array = [];
array.push(12345);
```

With bracket notation, the name of the method is now included in a string enclosed by square brackets, as in this example:

```
var array = [];
array["push"](12345);
```

This syntax is very useful when you want to dynamically decide which property to access. For example, here bracket notation allows you to use a variable instead of the string literal to specify the property to access.

```
var array = [];
var method = "push";
array[method](12345);
```

In this listing, the variable method has a value of "push", so push() is called on the array. This capability is quite useful, as you'll see throughout this book. The point to remember is that, other than syntax, the only difference—performance or otherwise—between dot notation and bracket notation is that bracket notation allows you to use special characters in property names. Developers tend to find dot notation easier to read, so you'll see it used more frequently than bracket notation.

Identifying Reference Types

A function is the easiest reference type to identify because when you use the typeof operator on a function, the operator should return "function":

```
function reflect(value) {
    return value;
}

console.log(typeof reflect);    // "function"
```

Other reference types are trickier to identify because, for all reference types other than functions, typeof returns "object". That's not very helpful when you're dealing with a lot of different types. To identify reference types more easily, you can use JavaScript's instanceof operator.

The instanceof operator takes an object and a constructor as parameters. When the value is an instance of the type that the constructor specifies, instanceof returns true; otherwise, it returns false, as you can see here:

```
var items = [];
var object = {};

function reflect(value) {
    return value;
}

console.log(items instanceof Array);        // true
console.log(object instanceof Object);      // true
console.log(reflect instanceof Function);   // true
```

In this example, several values are tested using `instanceof` and a constructor. Each reference type is correctly identified by using `instanceof` and the constructor that represents its true type (even though the constructor wasn't used in creating the variable).

The `instanceof` operator can identify inherited types. That means every object is actually an instance of `Object` because every reference type inherits from `Object`.

To demonstrate, the following listing examines the three references previously created with `instanceof`:

```
var items = [];
var object = {};

function reflect(value) {
    return value;
}

console.log(items instanceof Array);      // true
console.log(items instanceof Object);     // true
console.log(object instanceof Object);    // true
console.log(object instanceof Array);     // false
console.log(reflect instanceof Function); // true
console.log(reflect instanceof Object);   // true
```

Each reference type is correctly identified as an instance of `Object`, from which all reference types inherit.

Identifying Arrays

Although `instanceof` can identify arrays, there is one exception that affects web developers: JavaScript values can be passed back and forth between frames in the same web page. This becomes a problem only when you try to identify the type of a reference value, because each web page has its own global context—its own version of `Object`, `Array`, and all other built-in types. As a result, when you pass an array from one frame to another, `instanceof` doesn't work because the array is actually an instance of `Array` from a different frame.

To solve this problem, ECMAScript 5 introduced `Array.isArray()`, which definitively identifies the value as an instance of `Array` regardless of the value's origin. This method should return `true` when it receives a value that is a native array from any context. If your environment is ECMAScript 5 compliant, `Array.isArray()` is the best way to identify arrays:

```
var items = [];

console.log(Array.isArray(items));       // true
```

The `Array.isArray()` method is supported in most environments, both in browsers and in Node.js. This method isn't supported in Internet Explorer 8 and earlier.

Primitive Wrapper Types

Perhaps one of the most confusing parts of JavaScript is the concept of *primitive wrapper types.* There are three primitive wrapper types (`String`, `Number`, and `Boolean`). These special reference types exist to make working with primitive values as easy as working with objects. (It would be very confusing if you had to use a different syntax or switch to a procedural style just to get a substring of text.)

The primitive wrapper types are reference types that are automatically created behind the scenes whenever strings, numbers, or Booleans are read. For example, in the first line of this listing, a primitive string value is assigned to `name`. The second line treats `name` like an object and calls `charAt(0)` using dot notation.

```
var name = "Nicholas";
var firstChar = name.charAt(0);
console.log(firstChar);                 // "N"
```

This is what happens behind the scenes:

```
// what the JavaScript engine does
var name = "Nicholas";
var temp = new String(name);
var firstChar = temp.charAt(0);
temp = null;
console.log(firstChar);                 // "N"
```

Because the second line uses a string (a primitive) like an object, the JavaScript engine creates an instance of `String` so that `charAt(0)` will work. The `String` object exists only for one statement before it's destroyed (a process called *autoboxing*). To test this out, try adding a property to a string as if it were a regular object:

```
var name = "Nicholas";
name.last = "Zakas";

console.log(name.last);                 // undefined
```

This code attempts to add the property `last` to the string `name`. The code itself is just fine except that the property disappears. What happened? When working with regular objects, you can add properties at any time and they stay until you manually remove them. With primitive wrapper types, properties seem to disappear because the object on which the property was assigned is destroyed immediately afterward.

Here's what's actually happening in the JavaScript engine:

```javascript
// what the JavaScript engine does
var name = "Nicholas";
var temp = new String(name);
temp.last = "Zakas";
temp = null;                        // temporary object destroyed

var temp = new String(name);
console.log(temp.last);             // undefined
temp = null;
```

Instead of assigning a new property to a string, the code actually creates a new property on a temporary object that is then destroyed. When you try to access that property later, a different object is temporarily created and the new property doesn't exist there. Although reference values are created automatically for primitive values, when `instanceof` checks for these types of values the result is `false`:

```javascript
var name = "Nicholas";
var count = 10;
var found = false;

console.log(name instanceof String);    // false
console.log(count instanceof Number);    // false
console.log(found instanceof Boolean);   // false
```

The `instanceof` operator returns `false` because a temporary object is created only when a value is read. Because `instanceof` doesn't actually read anything, no temporary objects are created, and it tells us the values aren't instances of primitive wrapper types. You can create primitive wrapper types manually, but there are certain side effects:

```javascript
var name = new String("Nicholas");
var count = new Number(10);
var found = new Boolean(false);

console.log(typeof name);            // "object"
console.log(typeof count);           // "object"
console.log(typeof found);           // "object"
```

As you can see, creating an instance of the primitive wrapper type just creates another object, which means that `typeof` can't identify the type of data you intend to store.

In addition, you can't use `String`, `Number`, and `Boolean` objects as you would primitive values. For example, the following code uses a `Boolean` object. The `Boolean` object is `false`, yet `console.log("Found")` still executes because an object is always considered true inside a conditional statement. It doesn't matter that the object represents `false`; it's an object, so it evaluates to true.

```
var found = new Boolean(false);

if (found) {
    console.log("Found");        // this executes
}
```

Manually instantiating primitive wrappers can also be confusing in other ways, so unless you find a special case where it makes sense to do so, you should avoid it. Most of the time, using primitive wrapper objects instead of primitives only leads to errors.

Summary

While JavaScript doesn't have classes, it does have types. Each variable or piece of data is associated with a specific primitive or reference type. The five primitive types (strings, numbers, Booleans, null, and undefined) represent simple values stored directly in the variable object for a given context. You can use typeof to identify primitive types with the exception of null, which must be compared directly against the special value null.

Reference types are the closest thing to classes in JavaScript, and objects are instances of reference types. You can create new objects using the new operator or a reference literal. You access properties and methods primarily using dot notation, but you can also use bracket notation. Functions are objects in JavaScript, and you can identify them with the typeof operator. You should use instanceof with a constructor to identify objects of any other reference type.

To make primitives seem more like references, JavaScript has three primitive wrapper types: String, Number, and Boolean. JavaScript creates these objects behind the scenes so that you can treat primitives like regular objects, but the temporary objects are destroyed as soon as the statement using them is complete. Although you can create your own instances of primitive wrappers, it's best not to do that because it can be confusing.

2

FUNCTIONS

As discussed in Chapter 1, functions are actually objects in JavaScript. The defining characteristic of a function—what distinguishes it from any other object—is the presence of an *internal property* named [[Call]]. Internal properties are not accessible via code but rather define the behavior of code as it executes. ECMAScript defines multiple internal properties for objects in JavaScript, and these internal properties are indicated by double-square-bracket notation.

The [[Call]] property is unique to functions and indicates that the object can be executed. Because only functions have this property, the typeof operator is defined by ECMAScript to return "function" for any object with a [[Call]] property. That led to some confusion in the past, because some browsers also included a [[Call]] property for regular expressions, which were thus incorrectly identified as functions. All browsers now behave the same, so typeof no longer identifies regular expressions as functions.

This chapter discusses the various ways that functions are defined and executed in JavaScript. Because functions are objects, they behave differently than functions in other languages, and this behavior is central to a good understanding of JavaScript.

Declarations vs. Expressions

There are actually two literal forms of functions. The first is a *function declaration*, which begins with the function keyword and includes the name of the function immediately following it. The contents of the function are enclosed in braces, as shown in this declaration:

```
function add(num1, num2) {
    return num1 + num2;
}
```

The second form is a *function expression*, which doesn't require a name after function. These functions are considered anonymous because the function object itself has no name. Instead, function expressions are typically referenced via a variable or property, as in this expression:

```
var add = function(num1, num2) {
    return num1 + num2;
};
```

This code actually assigns a function value to the variable add. The function expression is almost identical to the function declaration except for the missing name and the semicolon at the end. Assignment expressions typically end with a semicolon, just as if you were assigning any other value.

Although these two forms are quite similar, they differ in a very important way. Function declarations are *hoisted* to the top of the context (either the function in which the declaration occurs or the global scope) when the code is executed. That means you can actually define a function after it is used in code without generating an error. For example:

```
var result = add(5, 5);

function add(num1, num2) {
    return num1 + num2;
}
```

This code might look like it will cause an error, but it works just fine. That's because the JavaScript engine hoists the function declaration to the top and actually executes the code as if it were written like this:

```
// how the JavaScript engine interprets the code
function add(num1, num2) {
    return num1 + num2;
}

var result = add(5, 5);
```

Function hoisting happens only for function declarations because the function name is known ahead of time. Function expressions, on the other hand, cannot be hoisted because the functions can be referenced only through a variable. So this code causes an error:

```
// error!
var result = add(5, 5);

var add = function(num1, num2) {
    return num1 + num2;
};
```

As long as you always define functions before using them, you can use either function declarations or function expressions.

Functions as Values

Because JavaScript has first-class functions, you can use them just as you do any other objects. You can assign them to variables, add them to objects, pass them to other functions as arguments, and return them from functions. Basically, you can use a function anywhere you would use any other reference value. This makes JavaScript functions incredibly powerful. Consider the following example:

```
❶ function sayHi() {
    console.log("Hi!");
}

sayHi();        // outputs "Hi!"

❷ var sayHi2 = sayHi;

sayHi2();       // outputs "Hi!"
```

In this code, there is a function declaration for sayHi ❶. A variable named sayHi2 is then created and assigned the value of sayHi ❷. Both sayHi and sayHi2 are now pointing to the same function, and that means either can be executed, with the same result. To understand why this happens, take a look at the same code rewritten to use the Function constructor:

```
var sayHi = new Function("console.log(\"Hi!\");");

sayHi();        // outputs "Hi!"

var sayHi2 = sayHi;

sayHi2();       // outputs "Hi!"
```

The Function constructor makes it more explicit that sayHi can be passed around just like any other object. When you keep in mind that functions are objects, a lot of the behavior starts to make sense.

For instance, you can pass a function into another function as an argument. The sort() method on JavaScript arrays accepts a comparison function as an optional parameter. The comparison function is called whenever two values in the array must be compared. If the first value is smaller than the second, the comparison function must return a negative number. If the first value is larger than the second, the function must return a positive number. If the two values are equal, the function should return zero.

By default, sort() converts every item in an array to a string and then performs a comparison. That means you can't accurately sort an array of numbers without specifying a comparison function. For example, you need to include a comparison function to accurately sort an array of numbers, such as:

```
  var numbers = [ 1, 5, 8, 4, 7, 10, 2, 6 ];
❶ numbers.sort(function(first, second) {
      return first - second;
  });

  console.log(numbers);       // "[1, 2, 4, 5, 6, 7, 8, 10]"

❷ numbers.sort();
  console.log(numbers);       // "[1, 10, 2, 4, 5, 6, 7, 8]"
```

In this example, the comparison function ❶ that is passed into sort() is actually a function expression. Note that there is no name for the function; it exists only as a reference that is passed into another function (making it an *anonymous function*). Subtracting the two values returns the correct result from the comparison function.

Compare that to the second call to sort() ❷, which does not use a comparison function. The order of the array is different than expected, as 1 is followed by 10. This is because the default comparison converts all values to strings before comparing them.

Parameters

Another unique aspect of JavaScript functions is that you can pass any number of parameters to any function without causing an error. That's because function parameters are actually stored as an array-like structure called arguments. Just like a regular JavaScript array, arguments can grow to contain any number of values. The values are referenced via numeric indices, and there is a length property to determine how many values are present.

The arguments object is automatically available inside any function. This means named parameters in a function exist mostly for convenience and don't actually limit the number of arguments that a function can accept.

NOTE *The arguments object is not an instance of Array and therefore doesn't have the same methods as an array; Array.isArray(arguments) always returns false.*

On the other hand, JavaScript doesn't ignore the named parameters of a function either. The number of arguments a function expects is stored on the function's length property. Remember, a function is actually just an object, so it can have properties. The length property indicates the function's *arity*, or the number of parameters it expects. Knowing the function's arity is important in JavaScript because functions won't throw an error if you pass in too many or too few parameters.

Here's a simple example using arguments and function arity; note that the number of arguments passed to the function has no effect on the reported arity:

```
function reflect(value) {
    return value;
}

console.log(reflect("Hi!"));        // "Hi!"
console.log(reflect("Hi!", 25));    // "Hi!"
console.log(reflect.length);        // 1

reflect = function() {
    return arguments[0];
};

console.log(reflect("Hi!"));        // "Hi!"
console.log(reflect("Hi!", 25));    // "Hi!"
console.log(reflect.length);        // 0
```

This example first defines the reflect() function using a single named parameter, but there is no error when a second parameter is passed into the function. Also, the length property is 1 because there is a single named parameter. The reflect() function is then redefined with no named parameters; it returns arguments[0], which is the first argument that is passed in. This new version of the function works exactly the same as the previous version, but its length is 0.

The first implementation of reflect() is much easier to understand because it uses a named argument (as you would in other languages). The version that uses the arguments object can be confusing because there are no named arguments, and you must read the body of the function to determine if arguments are used. That is why many developers prefer to avoid using arguments unless necessary.

Sometimes, however, using arguments is actually more effective than naming parameters. For instance, suppose you want to create a function that accepts any number of parameters and returns their sum. You can't use named parameters because you don't know how many you will need, so in this case, using arguments is the best option.

```
function sum() {

    var result = 0,
        i = 0,
        len = arguments.length;

    while (i < len) {
        result += arguments[i];
        i++;
    }

    return result;
}

console.log(sum(1, 2));          // 3
console.log(sum(3, 4, 5, 6));    // 18
console.log(sum(50));            // 50
console.log(sum());              // 0
```

The sum() function accepts any number of parameters and adds them together by iterating over the values in arguments with a while loop. This is exactly the same as if you had to add together an array of numbers. The function even works when no parameters are passed in, because result is initialized with a value of 0.

Overloading

Most object-oriented languages support *function overloading*, which is the ability of a single function to have multiple *signatures*. A function signature is made up of the function name plus the number and type of parameters the function expects. Thus, a single function can have one signature that accepts a single string argument and another that accepts two numeric arguments. The language determines which version of a function to call based on the arguments that are passed in.

As mentioned previously, JavaScript functions can accept any number of parameters, and the types of parameters a function takes aren't specified at all. That means JavaScript functions don't actually have signatures. A lack of function signatures also means a lack of function overloading. Look at what happens when you try to declare two functions with the same name:

```
function sayMessage(message) {
    console.log(message);
}

function sayMessage() {
    console.log("Default message");
}

sayMessage("Hello!");        // outputs "Default message"
```

If this were another language, the output of sayMessage("Hello!") would likely be "Hello!". In JavaScript, however, when you define multiple functions with the same name, the one that appears last in your code wins. The earlier function declarations are completely removed, and the last is the one that is used. Once again, it helps to think about this situation using objects:

```
var sayMessage = new Function("message", "console.log(message);");

sayMessage = new Function("console.log(\"Default message\");");

sayMessage("Hello!");        // outputs "Default message"
```

Looking at the code this way makes it clear why the previous code didn't work. A function object is being assigned to sayMessage twice in a row, so it makes sense that the first function object would be lost.

The fact that functions don't have signatures in JavaScript doesn't mean you can't mimic function overloading. You can retrieve the number of parameters that were passed in by using the arguments object, and you can use that information to determine what to do. For example:

```
function sayMessage(message) {

    if (arguments.length === 0) {
        message = "Default message";
    }

    console.log(message);
}

sayMessage("Hello!");        // outputs "Hello!"
```

In this example, the sayMessage() function behaves differently based on the number of parameters that were passed in. If no parameters are passed in (arguments.length === 0), then a default message is used. Otherwise, the first parameter is used as the message. This is a little more involved than function overloading in other languages, but the end result is the same. If you really want to check for different data types, you can use typeof and instanceof.

NOTE *In practice, checking the named parameter against undefined is more common than relying on arguments.length.*

Object Methods

As mentioned in Chapter 1, you can add and remove properties from objects at any time. When a property value is actually a function, the property is considered a method. You can add a method to an object in the same way that you would add a property. For example, in the following code, the person variable is assigned an object literal with a name property and a method called sayName.

```
var person = {
    name: "Nicholas",
    sayName: function() {
        console.log(person.name);
    }
};

person.sayName();        // outputs "Nicholas"
```

Note that the syntax for a data property and a method is exactly the same—an identifier followed by a colon and the value. In the case of sayName, the value just happens to be a function. You can then call the method directly from the object as in person.sayName("Nicholas").

The this Object

You may have noticed something strange in the previous example. The
sayName() method references person.name directly, which creates tight coupling between the method and the object. This is problematic for a number of reasons. First, if you change the variable name, you also need to
remember to change the reference to that name in the method. Second,
this sort of tight coupling makes it difficult to use the same function for
different objects. Fortunately, JavaScript has a way around this issue.

Every scope in JavaScript has a this object that represents the calling object for the function. In the global scope, this represents the
global object (window in web browsers). When a function is called while
attached to an object, the value of this is equal to that object by default.
So, instead of directly referencing an object inside a method, you can reference this instead. For example, you can rewrite the code from the previous example to use this:

```
var person = {
    name: "Nicholas",
    sayName: function() {
        console.log(this.name);
    }
};

person.sayName();        // outputs "Nicholas"
```

This code works the same as the earlier version, but this time, sayName()
references this instead of person. That means you can easily change the
name of the variable or even reuse the function on different objects.

```
function sayNameForAll() {
    console.log(this.name);
}

var person1 = {
    name: "Nicholas",
    sayName: sayNameForAll
};

var person2 = {
    name: "Greg",
    sayName: sayNameForAll
};

var name = "Michael";

person1.sayName();       // outputs "Nicholas"
person2.sayName();       // outputs "Greg"

sayNameForAll();         // outputs "Michael"
```

In this example, a function called sayName is defined first. Then, two object literals are created that assign sayName to be equal to the sayNameForAll function. Functions are just reference values, so you can assign them as property values on any number of objects. When sayName() is called on person1, it outputs "Nicholas"; when called on person2, it outputs "Greg". That's because this is set when the function is called, so this.name is accurate.

The last part of this example defines a global variable called name. When sayNameForAll() is called directly, it outputs "Michael" because the global variable is considered a property of the global object.

Changing this

The ability to use and manipulate the this value of functions is key to good object-oriented programming in JavaScript. Functions can be used in many different contexts, and they need to be able to work in each situation. Even though this is typically assigned automatically, you can change its value to achieve different goals. There are three function methods that allow you to change the value of this. (Remember that functions are objects, and objects can have methods, so functions can, too.)

The call() Method

The first function method for manipulating this is call(), which executes the function with a particular this value and with specific parameters. The first parameter of call() is the value to which this should be equal when the function is executed. All subsequent parameters are the parameters that should be passed into the function. For example, suppose you update sayNameForAll() to take a parameter:

```
function sayNameForAll(label) {
    console.log(label + ":" + this.name);
}

var person1 = {
    name: "Nicholas"
};

var person2 = {
    name: "Greg"
};

var name = "Michael";

sayNameForAll.call(this, "global");        // outputs "global:Michael"
sayNameForAll.call(person1, "person1");    // outputs "person1:Nicholas"
sayNameForAll.call(person2, "person2");    // outputs "person2:Greg"
```

In this example, sayNameForAll() accepts one parameter that is used as a label to the output value. The function is then called three times. Notice that there are no parentheses after the function name because it is accessed as an object rather than as code to execute. The first function call uses the global this and passes in the parameter "global" to output "global:Michael". The same function is called two more times, once each for person1 and person2. Because the call() method is being used, you don't need to add the function directly onto each object—you explicitly specify the value of this instead of letting the JavaScript engine do it automatically.

The apply() Method

The second function method you can use to manipulate this is apply(). The apply() method works exactly the same as call() except that it accepts only two parameters: the value for this and an array or array-like object of parameters to pass to the function (that means you can use an arguments object as the second parameter). So, instead of individually naming each parameter using call(), you can easily pass arrays to apply() as the second argument. Otherwise, call() and apply() behave identically. This example shows the apply() method in action:

```
function sayNameForAll(label) {
    console.log(label + ":" + this.name);
}

var person1 = {
    name: "Nicholas"
};

var person2 = {
    name: "Greg"
};

var name = "Michael";

sayNameForAll.apply(this, ["global"]);      // outputs "global:Michael"
sayNameForAll.apply(person1, ["person1"]);  // outputs "person1:Nicholas"
sayNameForAll.apply(person2, ["person2"]);  // outputs "person2:Greg"
```

This code takes the previous example and replaces call() with apply(); the result is exactly the same. The method you use typically depends on the type of data you have. If you already have an array of data, use apply(); if you just have individual variables, use call().

The bind() Method

The third function method for changing this is bind(). This method was added in ECMAScript 5, and it behaves quite differently than the other two. The first argument to bind() is the this value for the new function. All other arguments represent named parameters that should be permanently set in the new function. You can still pass in any parameters that aren't permanently set later.

The following code shows two examples that use bind(). You create the sayNameForPerson1() function by binding the this value to person1, while sayNameForPerson2() binds this to person2 and binds the first parameter as "person2".

```
function sayNameForAll(label) {
    console.log(label + ":" + this.name);
}

var person1 = {
    name: "Nicholas"
};

var person2 = {
    name: "Greg"
};

// create a function just for person1
❶ var sayNameForPerson1 = sayNameForAll.bind(person1);
sayNameForPerson1("person1");        // outputs "person1:Nicholas"

// create a function just for person2
❷ var sayNameForPerson2 = sayNameForAll.bind(person2, "person2");
sayNameForPerson2();                 // outputs "person2:Greg"

// attaching a method to an object doesn't change 'this'
❸ person2.sayName = sayNameForPerson1;
person2.sayName("person2");          // outputs "person2:Nicholas"
```

No parameters are bound for sayNameForPerson1() ❶, so you still need to pass in the label for the output. The function sayNameForPerson2() not only binds this to person2 but also binds the first parameter as "person2" ❷. That means you can call sayNameForPerson2() without passing in any additional arguments. The last part of this example adds sayNameForPerson1() onto person2 with the name sayName ❸. The function is bound, so the value of this doesn't change even though sayNameForPerson1 is now a function on person2. The method still outputs the value of person1.name.

Summary

JavaScript functions are unique in that they are also objects, meaning they can be accessed, copied, overwritten, and generally treated just like any other object value. The biggest difference between a JavaScript function and other objects is a special internal property, [[Call]], which contains the execution instructions for the function. The typeof operator looks for this internal property on an object, and if it finds it, returns "function".

There are two function literal forms: declarations and expressions. Function declarations contain the function name to the right of the function keyword and are hoisted to the top of the context in which they are defined. Function expressions are used where other values can also be used, such as assignment expressions, function parameters, or the return value of another function.

Because functions are objects, there is a Function constructor. You can create new functions with the Function constructor, but this isn't generally recommended because it can make your code harder to understand and debugging much more difficult. That said, you will likely run into its usage from time to time in situations where the true form of the function isn't known until runtime.

You need a good grasp of functions to understand how object-oriented programming works in JavaScript. Because JavaScript has no concept of a class, functions and other objects are all you have to work with to achieve aggregation and inheritance.

3

UNDERSTANDING OBJECTS

Even though there are a number of built-in reference types in JavaScript, you will most likely create your own objects fairly frequently. As you do so, keep in mind that objects in JavaScript are dynamic, meaning that they can change at any point during code execution. Whereas class-based languages lock down objects based on a class definition, JavaScript objects have no such restrictions.

A large part of JavaScript programming is managing those objects, which is why understanding how objects work is key to understanding JavaScript as a whole. This is discussed in more detail later in this chapter.

Defining Properties

Recall from Chapter 1 that there are two basic ways to create your own objects: using the `Object` constructor and using an object literal. For example:

```
var person1 = {
    name: "Nicholas"
};

var person2 = new Object();
person2.name = "Nicholas";

❶ person1.age = "Redacted";
  person2.age = "Redacted";

❷ person1.name = "Greg";
  person2.name = "Michael";
```

Both `person1` and `person2` are objects with a `name` property. Later in the example, both objects are assigned an age property ❶. You could do this immediately after the definition of the object or much later. Objects you create are always wide open for modification unless you specify otherwise (more on that in "Preventing Object Modification" on page 45). The last part of this example changes the value of `name` on each object ❷; property values can be changed at any time as well.

When a property is first added to an object, JavaScript uses an internal method called `[[Put]]` on the object. The `[[Put]]` method creates a spot in the object to store the property. You can compare this to adding a key to a hash table for the first time. This operation specifies not just the initial value, but also some attributes of the property. So, in the previous example, when the `name` and `age` properties are first defined on each object, the `[[Put]]` method is invoked for each.

The result of calling `[[Put]]` is the creation of an *own property* on the object. An own property simply indicates that the specific instance of the object owns that property. The property is stored directly on the instance, and all operations on the property must be performed through that object.

NOTE   *Own properties are distinct from* prototype properties, *which are discussed in Chapter 4.*

When a new value is assigned to an existing property, a separate operation called `[[Set]]` takes place. This operation replaces the current value of the property with the new one. In the previous example, setting `name` to a second value results in a call to [[Set]]. See Figure 3-1 for a step-by-step view of what happened to person1 behind the scenes as its name and age properties were changed.

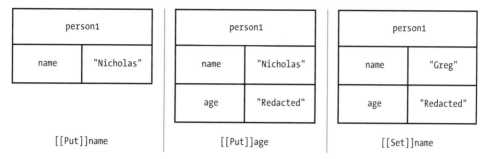

Figure 3-1: Adding and changing properties of an object

In the first part of the diagram, an object literal is used to create the person1 object. This performs an implicit [[Put]] for the name property. Assigning a value to person1.age performs a [[Put]] for the age property. However, setting person1.name to a new value ("Greg") performs a [[Set]] operation on the name property, overwriting the existing property value.

Detecting Properties

Because properties can be added at any time, it's sometimes necessary to check whether a property exists in the object. New JavaScript developers often incorrectly use patterns like the following to detect whether a property exists:

```
// unreliable
if (person1.age) {
    // do something with age
}
```

The problem with this pattern is how JavaScript's type coercion affects the outcome. The if condition evaluates to true if the value is *truthy* (an object, a nonempty string, a nonzero number, or true) and evaluates to false if the value is *falsy* (null, undefined, 0, false, NaN, or an empty string). Because an object property can contain one of these falsy values, the example code can yield false negatives. For instance, if person1.age is 0, then the if condition will not be met even though the property exists. A more reliable way to test for the existence of a property is with the in operator.

The in operator looks for a property with a given name in a specific object and returns true if it finds it. In effect, the in operator checks to see if the given key exists in the hash table. For example, here's what happens when in is used to check for some properties in the person1 object:

```
console.log("name" in person1);    // true
console.log("age" in person1);     // true
console.log("title" in person1);   // false
```

Keep in mind that methods are just properties that reference functions, so you can check for the existence of a method in the same way. The following adds a new function, sayName(), to person1 and uses in to confirm the function's presence.

```
var person1 = {
    name: "Nicholas",
    sayName: function() {
        console.log(this.name);
    }
};

console.log("sayName" in person1);  // true
```

In most cases, the in operator is the best way to determine whether the property exists in an object. It has the added benefit of not evaluating the value of the property, which can be important if such an evaluation is likely to cause a performance issue or an error.

In some cases, however, you might want to check for the existence of a property only if it is an own property. The in operator checks for both own properties and prototype properties, so you'll need to take a different approach. Enter the hasOwnProperty() method, which is present on all objects and returns true only if the given property exists and is an own property. For example, the following code compares the results of using in versus hasOwnProperty() on different properties in person1:

```
var person1 = {
    name: "Nicholas",
    sayName: function() {
        console.log(this.name);
    }
};

console.log("name" in person1);                     // true
console.log(person1.hasOwnProperty("name"));        // true

console.log("toString" in person1);                 // true
❶ console.log(person1.hasOwnProperty("toString"));   // false
```

In this example, `name` is an own property of `person1`, so both the `in` operator and `hasOwnProperty()` return true. The `toString()` method, however, is a prototype property that is present on all objects. The `in` operator returns `true` for `toString()`, but `hasOwnProperty()` returns false ❶. This is an important distinction that is discussed further in Chapter 4.

Removing Properties

Just as properties can be added to objects at any time, they can also be removed. Simply setting a property to `null` doesn't actually remove the property completely from the object, though. Such an operation calls [[Set]] with a value of `null`, which, as you saw earlier in the chapter, only replaces the value of the property. You need to use the `delete` operator to completely remove a property from an object.

The `delete` operator works on a single object property and calls an internal operation named [[Delete]]. You can think of this operation as removing a key/value pair from a hash table. When the `delete` operator is successful, it returns true. (Some properties can't be removed, and this is discussed in more detail later in the chapter.) For example, the following listing shows the `delete` operator at work:

```
var person1 = {
    name: "Nicholas"
};

console.log("name" in person1);      // true

delete person1.name;                 // true - not output
console.log("name" in person1);      // false
❶ console.log(person1.name);           // undefined
```

In this example, the `name` property is deleted from `person1`. The `in` operator returns `false` after the operation is complete. Also, note that attempting to access a property that doesn't exist will just return `undefined` ❶. Figure 3-2 shows how `delete` affects an object.

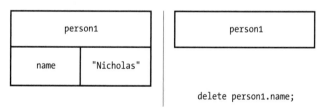

Figure 3-2: When you delete the name property, it completely disappears from person1.

Enumeration

By default, all properties that you add to an object are *enumerable*, which means that you can iterate over them using a for-in loop. Enumerable properties have their internal [[Enumerable]] attributes set to true. The for-in loop enumerates all enumerable properties on an object, assigning the property name to a variable. For example, the following loop outputs the property names and values of an object:

```
var property;

for (property in object) {
    console.log("Name: " + property);
    console.log("Value: " + object[property]);
}
```

Each time through the for-in loop, the property variable is filled with the next enumerable property on the object until all such properties have been used. At that point, the loop is finished and code execution continues. This example uses bracket notation to retrieve the value of the object property and output it to the console, which is one of the primary use cases for bracket notation in JavaScript.

If you just need a list of an object's properties to use later in your program, ECMAScript 5 introduced the Object.keys() method to retrieve an array of enumerable property names, as shown here:

```
❶ var properties = Object.keys(object);

// if you want to mimic for-in behavior
var i, len;

for (i=0, len=properties.length; i < len; i++){
    console.log("Name: " + properties[i]);
    console.log("Value: " + object[properties[i]]);
}
```

This example uses Object.keys() to retrieve the enumerable properties from an object ❶. A for loop is then used to iterate over the properties and output the name and value. Typically, you would use Object.keys() in situations where you want to operate on an array of property names and for-in when you don't need an array.

NOTE   *There is a difference between the enumerable properties returned in a for-in loop and the ones returned by Object.keys(). The for-in loop also enumerates prototype properties, while Object.keys() returns only own (instance) properties. The differences between prototype and own properties are discussed in Chapter 4.*

Keep in mind that not all properties are enumerable. In fact, most of the native methods on objects have their [[Enumerable]] attribute set to false. You can check whether a property is enumerable by using the propertyIsEnumerable() method, which is present on every object:

```
var person1 = {
    name: "Nicholas"
};

console.log("name" in person1);                            // true
❶ console.log(person1.propertyIsEnumerable("name"));        // true

var properties = Object.keys(person1);

console.log("length" in properties);                       // true
❷ console.log(properties.propertyIsEnumerable("length"));   // false
```

Here, the property name is enumerable, as it is a custom property defined on person1 ❶. The length property for the properties array, on the other hand, is not enumerable ❷ because it's a built-in property on Array.prototype. You'll find that many native properties are not enumerable by default.

Types of Properties

There are two different types of properties: data properties and accessor properties. *Data properties* contain a value, like the name property from earlier examples in this chapter. The default behavior of the [[Put]] method is to create a data property, and every example up to this point in the chapter has used data properties. *Accessor properties* don't contain a value but instead define a function to call when the property is read (called a *getter*), and a function to call when the property is written to (called a *setter*). Accessor properties only require either a getter or a setter, though they can have both.

There is a special syntax to define an accessor property using an object literal:

```
var person1 = {
❶   _name: "Nicholas",

❷   get name() {
        console.log("Reading name");
        return this._name;
    },
```

```
❸      set name(value) {
           console.log("Setting name to %s", value);
           this._name = value;
       }
   };

   console.log(person1.name);     // "Reading name" then "Nicholas"

   person1.name = "Greg";
   console.log(person1.name);     // "Setting name to Greg" then "Greg"
```

This example defines an accessor property called name. There is a data property called _name that contains the actual value for the property ❶. (The leading underscore is a common convention to indicate that the property is considered to be private, though in reality it is still public.) The syntax used to define the getter ❷ and setter ❸ for name looks a lot like a function but without the function keyword. The special keywords get and set are used before the accessor property name, followed by parentheses and a function body. Getters are expected to return a value, while setters receive the value being assigned to the property as an argument.

Even though this example uses _name to store the property data, you could just as easily store the data in a variable or even in another object. This example simply adds logging to the behavior of the property; there's usually no reason to use accessor properties if you are only storing the data in another property—just use the property itself. Accessor properties are most useful when you want the assignment of a value to trigger some sort of behavior, or when reading a value requires the calculation of the desired return value.

NOTE   *You don't need to define both a getter and a setter; you can choose one or both. If you define only a getter, then the property becomes read-only, and attempts to write to it will fail silently in nonstrict mode and throw an error in strict mode. If you define only a setter, then the property becomes write-only, and attempts to read the value will fail silently in both strict and nonstrict modes.*

Property Attributes

Prior to ECMAScript 5, there was no way to specify whether a property should be enumerable. In fact, there was no way to access the internal attributes of a property at all. ECMAScript 5 changed this by introducing several ways of interacting with property attributes directly, as well as introducing new attributes to support additional functionality. It's now possible to create properties that behave the same way as built-in JavaScript properties. This section covers in detail the attributes of both data and accessor properties, starting with the ones they have in common.

Common Attributes

There are two property attributes shared between data and accessor properties. One is [[Enumerable]], which determines whether you can iterate over the property. The other is [[Configurable]], which determines whether the property can be changed. You can remove a configurable property using delete and can change its attributes at any time. (This also means configurable properties can be changed from data to accessor properties and vice versa.) By default, all properties you declare on an object are both enumerable and configurable.

If you want to change property attributes, you can use the Object .defineProperty() method. This method accepts three arguments: the object that owns the property, the property name, and a *property descriptor* object containing the attributes to set. The descriptor has properties with the same name as the internal attributes but without the square brackets. So you use enumerable to set [[Enumerable]], and configurable to set [[Configurable]]. For example, suppose you want to make an object property nonenumerable and nonconfigurable:

```
   var person1 = {
❶     name: "Nicholas"
   };

   Object.defineProperty(person1, "name", {
❷     enumerable: false
   });

   console.log("name" in person1);                  // true
❸ console.log(person1.propertyIsEnumerable("name")); // false

   var properties = Object.keys(person1);
   console.log(properties.length);                   // 0

   Object.defineProperty(person1, "name", {
❹     configurable: false
   });

   // try to delete the Property
   delete person1.name;
❺ console.log("name" in person1);                   // true
   console.log(person1.name);                        // "Nicholas"

❻ Object.defineProperty(person1, "name", {          // error!!!
       configurable: true
   });
```

The name property is defined as usual ❶, but it's then modified to set its [[Enumerable]] attribute to false ❷. The propertyIsEnumerable() method now returns false ❸ because it references the new value of [[Enumerable]].

After that, name is changed to be nonconfigurable ❹. From now on, attempts to delete name fail because the property can't be changed, so name is still present on person1 ❺. Calling Object.defineProperty() on name again would also result in no further changes to the property. Effectively, name is locked down as a property on person1.

The last piece of the code tries to redefine name to be configurable once again ❻. However, this throws an error because you can't make a nonconfigurable property configurable again. Attempting to change a data property into an accessor property or vice versa should also throw an error in this case.

NOTE *When JavaScript is running in strict mode, attempting to delete a nonconfigurable property results in an error. In nonstrict mode, the operation silently fails.*

Data Property Attributes

Data properties possess two additional attributes that accessors do not. The first is [[Value]], which holds the property value. This attribute is filled in automatically when you create a property on an object. All property values are stored in [[Value]], even if the value is a function.

The second attribute is [[Writable]], which is a Boolean value indicating whether the property can be written to. By default, all properties are writable unless you specify otherwise.

With these two additional attributes, you can fully define a data property using Object.defineProperty() even if the property doesn't already exist. Consider this code:

```
var person1 = {
    name: "Nicholas"
};
```

You've seen this snippet throughout this chapter; it adds the name property to person1 and sets its value. You can achieve the same result using the following (more verbose) code:

```
var person1 = {};

Object.defineProperty(person1, "name", {
    value: "Nicholas",
    enumerable: true,
    configurable: true,
    writable: true
});
```

When `Object.defineProperty()` is called, it first checks to see if the property exists. If the property doesn't exist, a new one is added with the attributes specified in the descriptor. In this case, `name` isn't already a property of `person1`, so it is created.

When you are defining a new property with `Object.defineProperty()`, it's important to specify all of the attributes because Boolean attributes automatically default to `false` otherwise. For example, the following code creates a `name` property that is nonenumerable, nonconfigurable, and nonwritable because it doesn't explicitly make any of those attributes `true` in the call to `Object.defineProperty()`.

```
var person1 = {};

Object.defineProperty(person1, "name", {
    value: "Nicholas"
});

console.log("name" in person1);                     // true
console.log(person1.propertyIsEnumerable("name"));  // false

delete person1.name;
console.log("name" in person1);                     // true

person1.name = "Greg";
console.log(person1.name);                          // "Nicholas"
```

In this code, you can't do anything with the `name` property except read the value; every other operation is locked down. If you're changing an existing property, keep in mind that only the attributes you specify will change.

NOTE *Nonwritable properties throw an error in strict mode when you try to change the value. In nonstrict mode, the operation silently fails.*

Accessor Property Attributes

Accessor properties also have two additional attributes. Because there is no value stored for accessor properties, there is no need for `[[Value]]` or `[[Writable]]`. Instead, accessors have `[[Get]]` and `[[Set]]`, which contain the getter and setter functions, respectively. As with the object literal form of getters and setters, you need only define one of these attributes to create the property.

NOTE *If you try to create a property with both data and accessor attributes, you will get an error.*

The advantage of using accessor property attributes instead of object literal notation to define accessor properties is that you can also define those properties on existing objects. If you want to use object literal notation, you have to define accessor properties when you create the object.

As with data properties, you can also specify whether accessor properties are configurable or enumerable. Consider this example from earlier:

```
var person1 = {
    _name: "Nicholas",

    get name() {
        console.log("Reading name");
        return this._name;
    },

    set name(value) {
        console.log("Setting name to %s", value);
        this._name = value;
    }
};
```

This code can also be written as follows:

```
var person1 = {
    _name: "Nicholas"
};

Object.defineProperty(person1, "name", {
    get: function() {
        console.log("Reading name");
        return this._name;
    },
    set: function(value) {
        console.log("Setting name to %s", value);
        this._name = value;
    },
    enumerable: true,
    configurable: true
});
```

Notice that the get and set keys on the object passed in to Object .defineProperty() are data properties that contain a function. You can't use object literal accessor format here.

Setting the other attributes ([[Enumerable]] and [[Configurable]]) allows you to change how the accessor property works. For example, you can create a nonconfigurable, nonenumerable, nonwritable property like this:

```
var person1 = {
    _name: "Nicholas"
};
```

```
    Object.defineProperty(person1, "name", {
        get: function() {
            console.log("Reading name");
❶           return this._name;
        }
    });
```

```
    console.log("name" in person1);                    // true
    console.log(person1.propertyIsEnumerable("name")); // false
    delete person1.name;
    console.log("name" in person1);                    // true

    person1.name = "Greg";
    console.log(person1.name);                         // "Nicholas"
```

In this code, the name property is an accessor property with only a getter ❶. There is no setter or any other attributes to explicitly set to true, so the value can be read but not changed.

NOTE   *As with accessor properties defined via object literal notation, an accessor property without a setter throws an error in strict mode when you try to change the value. In nonstrict mode, the operation silently fails. Attempting to read an accessor property that has only a setter defined always returns undefined.*

Defining Multiple Properties

It's also possible to define multiple properties on an object simultaneously if you use Object.defineProperties() instead of Object.defineProperty(). This method accepts two arguments: the object to work on and an object containing all of the property information. The keys of that second argument are property names, and the values are descriptor objects defining the attributes for those properties. For example, the following code defines two properties:

```
    var person1 = {};

    Object.defineProperties(person1, {

❶       // data property to store data
        _name: {
            value: "Nicholas",
            enumerable: true,
            configurable: true,
            writable: true
        },
```

```
❷     // accessor property
    name: {
        get: function() {
            console.log("Reading name");
            return this._name;
        },
        set: function(value) {
            console.log("Setting name to %s", value);
            this._name = value;
        },
        enumerable: true,
        configurable: true
    }
});
```

This example defines _name as a data property to contain information ❶ and name as an accessor property ❷. You can define any number
of properties using Object.defineProperties(); you can even change existing
properties and create new ones at the same time. The effect is the same
as calling Object.defineProperty() multiple times.

Retrieving Property Attributes

If you need to fetch property attributes, you can do so in JavaScript by
using Object.getOwnPropertyDescriptor(). As the name suggests, this method
works only on own properties. This method accepts two arguments: the
object to work on and the property name to retrieve. If the property exists,
you should receive a descriptor object with four properties: configurable,
enumerable, and the two others appropriate for the type of property. Even
if you didn't specifically set an attribute, you will still receive an object
containing the appropriate value for that attribute. For example, this
code creates a property and checks its attributes:

```
var person1 = {
    name: "Nicholas"
};

var descriptor = Object.getOwnPropertyDescriptor(person1, "name");

console.log(descriptor.enumerable);     // true
console.log(descriptor.configurable);   // true
console.log(descriptor.writable);       // true
console.log(descriptor.value);          // "Nicholas"
```

Here, a property called name is defined as part of an object literal. The
call to Object.getOwnPropertyDescriptor() returns an object with enumerable,
configurable, writable, and value, even though these weren't explicitly
defined via Object.defineProperty().

Preventing Object Modification

Objects, just like properties, have internal attributes that govern their behavior. One of these attributes is [[Extensible]], which is a Boolean value indicating if the object itself can be modified. All objects you create are *extensible* by default, meaning new properties can be added to the object at any time. You've seen this several times in this chapter. By setting [[Extensible]] to false, you can prevent new properties from being added to an object. There are three different ways to accomplish this.

Preventing Extensions

One way to create a nonextensible object is with Object.preventExtensions(). This method accepts a single argument, which is the object you want to make nonextensible. Once you use this method on an object, you'll never be able to add any new properties to it again. You can check the value of [[Extensible]] by using Object.isExtensible(). The following code shows examples of both methods at work.

```
var person1 = {
    name: "Nicholas"
};

❶ console.log(Object.isExtensible(person1));        // true

❷ Object.preventExtensions(person1);
  console.log(Object.isExtensible(person1));        // false

❸ person1.sayName = function() {
      console.log(this.name);
  };

  console.log("sayName" in person1);                // false
```

After creating person1, this example checks the object's [[Extensible]] attribute ❶ before making it unchangeable ❷. Now that person1 is non-extensible, the sayName() method ❸ is never added to it.

NOTE   *Attempting to add a property to a nonextensible object will throw an error in strict mode. In nonstrict mode, the operation fails silently. You should always use strict mode with nonextensible objects so that you are aware when a nonextensible object is being used incorrectly.*

Sealing Objects

The second way to create a nonextensible object is to *seal* the object. A sealed object is nonextensible, and all of its properties are nonconfigurable. That means not only can you not add new properties to the object, but you also can't remove properties or change their type (from data to accessor or vice versa). If an object is sealed, you can only read from and write to its properties.

You can use the Object.seal() method on an object to seal it. When that happens, the [[Extensible]] attribute is set to false, and all properties have their [[Configurable]] attribute set to false. You can check to see whether an object is sealed using Object.isSealed() as follows:

```
var person1 = {
    name: "Nicholas"
};

console.log(Object.isExtensible(person1));      // true
console.log(Object.isSealed(person1));          // false

❶ Object.seal(person1);
❷ console.log(Object.isExtensible(person1));      // false
  console.log(Object.isSealed(person1));          // true

❸ person1.sayName = function() {
      console.log(this.name);
  };

  console.log("sayName" in person1);              // false

❹ person1.name = "Greg";
  console.log(person1.name);                      // "Greg"

❺ delete person1.name;
  console.log("name" in person1);                 // true
  console.log(person1.name);                      // "Greg"

  var descriptor = Object.getOwnPropertyDescriptor(person1, "name");
  console.log(descriptor.configurable);           // false
```

This code seals person1 ❶ so you can't add or remove properties. Since all sealed objects are nonextensible, Object.isExtensible() returns false ❷ when used on person1, and the attempt to add a method called sayName() ❸ fails silently. Also, though person1.name is successfully changed to a new value ❹, the attempt to delete it ❺ fails.

If you're familiar with Java or C++, sealed objects should also be familiar. When you create a new object instance based on a class in one of those languages, you can't add any new properties to that object. However, if a property contains an object, you can modify that object. In effect, sealed objects are JavaScript's way of giving you the same measure of control without using classes.

NOTE   *Be sure to use strict mode with sealed objects so you'll get an error when someone tries to use the object incorrectly.*

Freezing Objects

The last way to create a nonextensible object is to *freeze* it. If an object is frozen, you can't add or remove properties, you can't change properties' types, and you can't write to any data properties. In essence, a frozen object is a sealed object where data properties are also read-only. Frozen objects can't become unfrozen, so they remain in the state they were in when they became frozen. You can freeze an object by using `Object.freeze()` and determine if an object is frozen by using `Object.isFrozen()`. For example:

```
var person1 = {
    name: "Nicholas"
};

console.log(Object.isExtensible(person1));    // true
console.log(Object.isSealed(person1));        // false
console.log(Object.isFrozen(person1));        // false

❶ Object.freeze(person1);
❷ console.log(Object.isExtensible(person1));    // false
❸ console.log(Object.isSealed(person1));        // true
  console.log(Object.isFrozen(person1));        // true

person1.sayName = function() {
    console.log(this.name);
};

console.log("sayName" in person1);            // false

❹ person1.name = "Greg";
  console.log(person1.name);                    // "Nicholas"

delete person1.name;
console.log("name" in person1);               // true
console.log(person1.name);                    // "Nicholas"

var descriptor = Object.getOwnPropertyDescriptor(person1, "name");
console.log(descriptor.configurable);         // false
console.log(descriptor.writable);             // false
```

In this example, person1 is frozen ❶. Frozen objects are also considered nonextensible and sealed, so `Object.isExtensible()` returns false ❷ and `Object.isSealed()` returns true ❸. The name property can't be changed, so even though it is assigned to "Greg", the operation fails ❹, and subsequent checks of name will still return "Nicholas".

NOTE *Frozen objects are simply snapshots of an object at a particular point in time. They are of limited use and should be used rarely. As with all nonextensible objects, you should use strict mode with frozen objects.*

Summary

It helps to think of JavaScript objects as hash maps where properties are just key/value pairs. You access object properties using either dot notation or bracket notation with a string identifier. You can add a property at any time by assigning a value to it, and you can remove a property at any time with the delete operator. You can always check whether a property exists by using the in operator on a property name and object. If the property in question is an own property, you could also use hasOwnProperty(), which exists on every object. All object properties are enumerable by default, which means that they will appear in a for-in loop or be retrieved by Object.keys().

There are two types of properties: data properties and accessor properties. Data properties are placeholders for values, and you can read from and write to them. When a data property holds a function value, the property is considered a method of the object. Unlike data properties, accessor properties don't store values on their own; they use a combination of getters and setters to perform specific actions. You can create both data properties and accessor properties directly using object literal notation.

All properties have several associated attributes. These attributes define how the properties work. Both data and accessor properties have [[Enumerable]] and [[Configurable]] attributes. Data properties also have [[Writable]] and [[Value]] attributes, while accessor properties have [[Get]] and [[Set]] attributes. By default, [[Enumerable]] and [[Configurable]] are set to true for all properties, and [[Writable]] is set to true for data properties. You can change these attributes by using Object.defineProperty() or Object.defineProperties(). It's also possible to retrieve these attributes by using Object.getOwnPropertyDescriptor().

When you want to lock down an object's properties in some way, there are three different ways to do so. If you use Object.preventExtensions(), objects will no longer allow properties to be added. You could also create a sealed object with the Object.seal() method, which makes that object nonextensible and makes its properties nonconfigurable. The Object.freeze() method creates a frozen object, which is a sealed object with nonwritable data properties. Be careful with nonextensible objects, and always use strict mode so that attempts to access the objects incorrectly will throw an error.

4

CONSTRUCTORS AND PROTOTYPES

You might be able to get pretty far in JavaScript without understanding constructors and prototypes, but you won't truly appreciate the language without a good grasp of them. Because JavaScript lacks classes, it turns to constructors and prototypes to bring a similar order to objects. But just because some of the patterns resemble classes doesn't mean they behave the same way. In this chapter, you'll explore constructors and prototypes in detail to see how JavaScript uses them to create objects.

Constructors

A *constructor* is simply a function that is used with new to create an object. Up to this point, you've seen several of the built-in JavaScript constructors, such as Object, Array, and Function. The advantage of constructors is that objects created with the same constructor contain the same properties and methods. If you want to create multiple similar objects, you can create your own constructors and therefore your own reference types.

Because a constructor is just a function, you define it in the same way. The only difference is that constructor names should begin with a capital letter, to distinguish them from other functions. For example, look at the following empty `Person` function:

```
function Person() {
    // intentionally empty
}
```

This function is a constructor, but there is absolutely no syntactic difference between this and any other function. The clue that `Person` is a constructor is in the name—the first letter is capitalized.

After the constructor is defined, you can start creating instances, like the following two `Person` objects:

```
var person1 = new Person();
var person2 = new Person();
```

When you have no parameters to pass into your constructor, you can even omit the parentheses:

```
var person1 = new Person;
var person2 = new Person;
```

Even though the `Person` constructor doesn't explicitly return anything, both `person1` and `person2` are considered instances of the new `Person` type. The `new` operator automatically creates an object of the given type and returns it. That also means you can use the `instanceof` operator to deduce an object's type. The following code shows `instanceof` in action with the newly created objects:

```
console.log(person1 instanceof Person);    // true
console.log(person2 instanceof Person);    // true
```

Because `person1` and `person2` were created with the `Person` constructor, `instanceof` returns true when it checks whether these objects are instances of the `Person` type.

You can also check the type of an instance using the `constructor` property. Every object instance is automatically created with a `constructor` property that contains a reference to the constructor function that created it. For *generic* objects (those created via an object literal or the `Object` constructor), `constructor` is set to `Object`; for objects created with a custom constructor, constructor points back to that constructor function instead. For example, `Person` is the constructor property for `person1` and `person2`:

```
console.log(person1.constructor === Person);    // true
console.log(person2.constructor === Person);    // true
```

The `console.log` function outputs `true` in both cases, because both objects were created with the `Person` constructor.

Even though this relationship exists between an instance and its constructor, you are still advised to use `instanceof` to check the type of an instance. This is because the constructor property can be overwritten and therefore may not be completely accurate.

Of course, an empty constructor function isn't very useful. The whole point of a constructor is to make it easy to create more objects with the same properties and methods. To do that, simply add any properties you want to this inside of the constructor, as in the following example:

```
  function Person(name) {
❶     this.name = name;
❷     this.sayName = function() {
          console.log(this.name);
      };
  }
```

This version of the `Person` constructor accepts a single named parameter, `name`, and assigns it to the `name` property of the this object ❶. The constructor also adds a `sayName()` method to the object ❷. The this object is automatically created by `new` when you call the constructor, and it is an instance of the constructor's type. (In this case, this is an instance of `Person`.) There's no need to return a value from the function because the `new` operator produces the return value.

Now you can use the `Person` constructor to create objects with an initialized `name` property:

```
var person1 = new Person("Nicholas");
var person2 = new Person("Greg");

console.log(person1.name);          // "Nicholas"
console.log(person2.name);          // "Greg"

person1.sayName();                  // outputs "Nicholas"
person2.sayName();                  // outputs "Greg"
```

Each object has its own `name` property, so `sayName()` should return different values depending on the object on which you use it.

You can also explicitly call return *inside of a constructor. If the returned value is an object, it will be returned instead of the newly created object instance. If the returned value is a primitive, the newly created object is used and the returned value is ignored.*

Constructors allow you to initialize an instance of a type in a consistent way, performing all of the property setup that is necessary before the object can be used. For example, you could also use Object .defineProperty() inside of a constructor to help initialize the instance:

```
function Person(name) {

    Object.defineProperty(this, "name", {
        get: function() {
            return name;
        },
        set: function(newName) {
            name = newName;
        },
        enumerable: true,
        configurable: true
    });

    this.sayName = function() {
        console.log(this.name);
    };
}
```

In this version of the Person constructor, the name property is an accessor property that uses the name parameter for storing the actual name. This is possible because named parameters act like local variables.

Make sure to always call constructors with new; otherwise, you risk changing the global object instead of the newly created object. Consider what happens in the following code:

```
var person1 = Person("Nicholas");         // note: missing "new"

console.log(person1 instanceof Person);   // false
console.log(typeof person1);              // "undefined"
console.log(name);                        // "Nicholas"
```

When Person is called as a function without new, the value of this inside of the constructor is equal to the global this object. The variable person1 doesn't contain a value because the Person constructor relies on new to supply a return value. Without new, Person is just a function without a return statement. The assignment to this.name actually creates a global variable called name, which is where the name passed to Person is stored. Chapter 6 describes a solution to both this problem and more complex object composition patterns.

NOTE   *An error occurs if you call the Person constructor in strict mode without using new. This is because strict mode doesn't assign this to the global object. Instead, this remains undefined, and an error occurs whenever you attempt to create a property on undefined.*

Constructors allow you to configure object instances with the same properties, but constructors alone don't eliminate code redundancy. In the example code thus far, each instance has had its own sayName() method even though sayName() doesn't change. That means if you have 100 instances of an object, then there are 100 copies of a function that do the exact same thing, just with different data.

It would be much more efficient if all of the instances shared one method, and then that method could use this.name to retrieve the appropriate data. This is where prototypes come in.

Prototypes

You can think of a *prototype* as a recipe for an object. Almost every function (with the exception of some built-in functions) has a prototype property that is used during the creation of new instances. That prototype is shared among all of the object instances, and those instances can access properties of the prototype. For example, the hasOwnProperty() method is defined on the generic Object prototype, but it can be accessed from any object as if it were an own property, as shown in this example:

```
var book = {
    title: "The Principles of Object-Oriented JavaScript"
};

console.log("title" in book);                                 // true
console.log(book.hasOwnProperty("title"));                    // true
console.log("hasOwnProperty" in book);                        // true
console.log(book.hasOwnProperty("hasOwnProperty"));           // false
console.log(Object.prototype.hasOwnProperty("hasOwnProperty")); // true
```

Even though there is no definition for hasOwnProperty() on book, that method can still be accessed as book.hasOwnProperty() because the definition does exist on Object.prototype. Remember that the in operator returns true for both prototype properties *and* own properties.

The [[Prototype]] Property

An instance keeps track of its prototype through an internal property called [[Prototype]]. This property is a pointer back to the prototype object that the instance is using. When you create a new object using new, the constructor's prototype property is assigned to the [[Prototype]] property of that new object. Figure 4-1 shows how the [[Prototype]] property lets multiple instances of an object type refer to the same prototype, which can reduce code duplication.

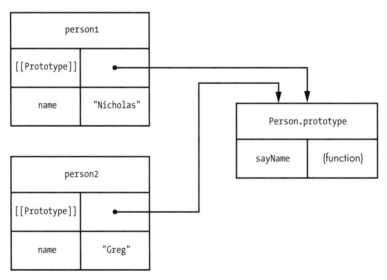

Figure 4-1: The [[Prototype]] properties for person1 and person2 point to the same prototype.

You can read the value of the [[Prototype]] property by using the Object.getPrototypeOf() method on an object. For example, the following code checks the [[Prototype]] of a generic, empty object.

```
❶ var object = {};
  var prototype = Object.getPrototypeOf(object);

  console.log(prototype === Object.prototype);          // true
```

For any generic object like this one ❶, [[Prototype]] is always a reference to Object.prototype.

Some JavaScript engines also support a property called __proto__ on all objects. This property allows you to both read from and write to the [[Prototype]] property. Firefox, Safari, Chrome, and Node.js all support this property, and __proto__ is on the path for standardization in ECMAScript 6.

You can also test to see if one object is a prototype for another by using the isPrototypeOf() method, which is included on all objects:

```
var object = {};

console.log(Object.prototype.isPrototypeOf(object));     // true
```

Because object is just a generic object, its prototype should be Object .prototype, meaning isPrototypeOf() should return true.

When a property is read on an object, the JavaScript engine first looks for an own property with that name. If the engine finds a correctly named own property, it returns that value. If no own property with that name exists on the target object, JavaScript searches the [[Prototype]] object instead. If a prototype property with that name exists, the value of that property is returned. If the search concludes without finding a property with the correct name, undefined is returned.

Consider the following, in which an object is first created without any own properties:

```
  var object = {};

❶ console.log(object.toString());     // "[object Object]"

  object.toString = function() {
      return "[object Custom]";
  };

❷ console.log(object.toString());     // "[object Custom]"

  // delete own property
  delete object.toString;
```

```
❸ console.log(object.toString());    // "[object Object]"

// no effect - delete only works on own properties
delete object.toString;
console.log(object.toString());    // "[object Object]"
```

In this example, the toString() method comes from the prototype and
returns "[object Object]" ❶ by default. If you then define an own property
called toString(), that own property is used whenever toString() is called
on the object again ❷. The own property *shadows* the prototype property,
so the prototype property of the same name is no longer used. The prototype property is used again only if the own property is deleted from the
object ❸. (Keep in mind that you can't delete a prototype property from
an instance because the delete operator acts only on own properties.)
Figure 4-2 shows what is happening in this example.

This example also highlights an important concept: You cannot
assign a value to a prototype property from an instance. As you can see
in the middle section of Figure 4-2, assigning a value to toString creates a
new own property on the instance, leaving the property on the prototype
untouched.

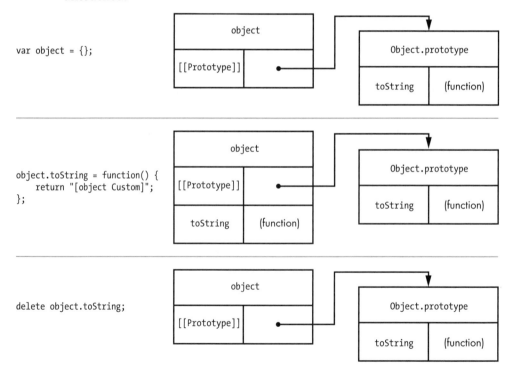

*Figure 4-2: An object with no own properties (top) has only the methods of its prototype. Adding a
toString() property to the object (middle) replaces the prototype property until you delete it (bottom).*

Using Prototypes with Constructors

The shared nature of prototypes makes them ideal for defining methods once for all objects of a given type. Because methods tend to do the same thing for all instances, there's no reason each instance needs its own set of methods.

It's much more efficient to put the methods on the prototype and then use this to access the current instance. For example, consider the following new Person constructor:

```
function Person(name) {
    this.name = name;
}

❶ Person.prototype.sayName = function() {
    console.log(this.name);
};

var person1 = new Person("Nicholas");
var person2 = new Person("Greg");

console.log(person1.name);          // "Nicholas"
console.log(person2.name);          // "Greg"

person1.sayName();                  // outputs "Nicholas"
person2.sayName();                  // outputs "Greg"
```

In this version of the Person constructor, sayName() is defined on the prototype ❶ instead of in the constructor. The object instances work exactly the same as the example from earlier in this chapter, even though sayName() is now a prototype property instead of an own property. Because person1 and person2 are each base references for their calls to sayName(), the this value is assigned to person1 and person2, respectively.

You can also store other types of data on the prototype, but be careful when using reference values. Because these values are shared across instances, you might not expect one instance to be able to change values that another instance will access. This example shows what can happen when you don't watch where your reference values are pointing:

```
function Person(name) {
    this.name = name;
}

Person.prototype.sayName = function() {
    console.log(this.name);
};
```

```
❶ Person.prototype.favorites = [];

  var person1 = new Person("Nicholas");
  var person2 = new Person("Greg");

  person1.favorites.push("pizza");
  person2.favorites.push("quinoa");

  console.log(person1.favorites);      // "pizza,quinoa"
  console.log(person2.favorites);      // "pizza,quinoa"
```

The favorites property ❶ is defined on the prototype, which means person1.favorites and person2.favorites point to the *same array*. Any values you add to either person's favorites will be elements in that array on the prototype. That may not be the behavior that you actually want, so it's important to be very careful about what you define on the prototype.

Even though you can add properties to the prototype one by one, many developers use a more succinct pattern that involves replacing the prototype with an object literal:

```
  function Person(name) {
      this.name = name;
  }

  Person.prototype = {
❶     sayName: function() {
          console.log(this.name);
      },

❷     toString: function() {
          return "[Person " + this.name + "]";
      }
  };
```

This code defines two methods on the prototype, sayName() ❶ and toString() ❷. This pattern has become quite popular because it eliminates the need to type Person.prototype multiple times. There is, however, one side effect to be aware of:

```
  var person1 = new Person("Nicholas");

  console.log(person1 instanceof Person);         // true
  console.log(person1.constructor === Person);    // false
❶ console.log(person1.constructor === Object);    // true
```

Using the object literal notation to overwrite the prototype changed the constructor property so that it now points to Object ❶ instead of Person. This happened because the constructor property exists on the prototype, not on the object instance. When a function is created, its prototype property is created with a constructor property equal to the function. This pattern completely overwrites the prototype object, which means that constructor will come from the newly created (generic) object that was assigned to Person.prototype. To avoid this, restore the constructor property to a proper value when overwriting the prototype:

```
function Person(name) {
    this.name = name;
}

Person.prototype = {
❶   constructor: Person,

    sayName: function() {
        console.log(this.name);
    },

    toString: function() {
        return "[Person " + this.name + "]";
    }
};

var person1 = new Person("Nicholas");
var person2 = new Person("Greg");

console.log(person1 instanceof Person);        // true
console.log(person1.constructor === Person);   // true
console.log(person1.constructor === Object);   // false

console.log(person2 instanceof Person);        // true
console.log(person2.constructor === Person);   // true
console.log(person2.constructor === Object);   // false
```

In this example, the constructor property is specifically assigned on the prototype ❶. It's good practice to make this the first property on the prototype so you don't forget to include it.

Perhaps the most interesting aspect of the relationships among constructors, prototypes, and instances is that there is no direct link between the instance and the constructor. There is, however, a direct link between the instance and the prototype and between the prototype and the constructor. Figure 4-3 illustrates this relationship.

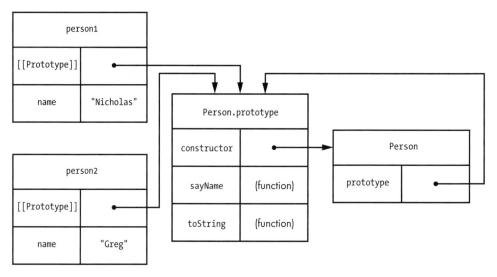

Figure 4-3: An instance and its constructor are linked via the prototype.

This nature of this relationship means that any disruption between the instance and the prototype will also create a disruption between the instance and the constructor.

Changing Prototypes

Because all instances of a particular type reference a shared prototype, you can augment all of those objects together at any time. Remember, the [[Prototype]] property just contains a pointer to the prototype, and any changes to the prototype are immediately available on any instance referencing it. That means you can literally add new members to a prototype at any point and have those changes reflected on existing instances, as in this example:

```
function Person(name) {
    this.name = name;
}

Person.prototype = {
    constructor: Person,

❶   sayName: function() {
        console.log(this.name);
    },

❷   toString: function() {
        return "[Person " + this.name + "]";
    }
};
```

```
❸ var person1 = new Person("Nicholas");
   var person2 = new Person("Greg");

   console.log("sayHi" in person1);        // false
   console.log("sayHi" in person2);        // false

   // add a new method
❹ Person.prototype.sayHi = function() {
       console.log("Hi");
   };

❺ person1.sayHi();                         // outputs "Hi"
   person2.sayHi();                         // outputs "Hi"
```

In this code, the Person type starts out with only two methods, sayName() ❶ and toString() ❷. Two instances of Person are created ❸, and then the sayHi() ❹ method is added to the prototype. After that point, both instances can now access sayHi() ❺. The search for a named property happens each time that property is accessed, so the experience is seamless.

The ability to modify the prototype at any time has some interesting repercussions for sealed and frozen objects. When you use Object.seal() or Object.freeze() on an object, you are acting *solely* on the object instance and the own properties. You can't add new own properties or change existing own properties on frozen objects, but you can certainly still add properties on the prototype and continue extending those objects, as demonstrated in the following listing.

```
   var person1 = new Person("Nicholas");
   var person2 = new Person("Greg");

❶ Object.freeze(person1);

❷ Person.prototype.sayHi = function() {
       console.log("Hi");
   };

   person1.sayHi();                         // outputs "Hi"
   person2.sayHi();                         // outputs "Hi"
```

In this example, there are two instances of Person. The first (person1) is frozen ❶, while the second is a normal object. When you add sayHi() to the prototype ❷, both person1 and person2 attain a new method, seemingly contradicting person1's frozen status. The [[Prototype]] property is considered an own property of the instance, and while the property itself is frozen, the value (an object) is not.

In practice, you probably won't use prototypes this way very often when developing in JavaScript. However, it's important to understand the relationships that exist between objects and their prototype, and strange examples like this help to illuminate the concepts.

Built-in Object Prototypes

At this point, you might wonder if prototypes also allow you to modify the built-in objects that come standard in the JavaScript engine. The answer is yes. All built-in objects have constructors, and therefore, they have prototypes that you can change. For instance, adding a new method for use on all arrays is as simple as modifying `Array.prototype`.

```
Array.prototype.sum = function() {
    return this.reduce(function(previous, current) {
        return previous + current;
    });
};

var numbers = [ 1, 2, 3, 4, 5, 6 ];
var result = numbers.sum();

console.log(result);                    // 21
```

This example creates a method called `sum()` on `Array.prototype` that simply adds up all of the items in the array and returns the result. The `numbers` array automatically has access to that method through the prototype. Inside of `sum()`, this refers to `numbers`, which is an instance of `Array`, so the method is free to use other array methods such as `reduce()`.

You may recall that strings, numbers, and Booleans all have built-in primitive wrapper types that are used to access primitive values as if they were objects. If you modify the primitive wrapper type prototype as in this example, you can actually add more functionality to those primitive values:

```
String.prototype.capitalize = function() {
    return this.charAt(0).toUpperCase() + this.substring(1);
};

var message = "hello world!";
console.log(message.capitalize());  // "Hello world!"
```

This code creates a new method called `capitalize()` for strings. The `String` type is the primitive wrapper for strings, and modifying its prototype means that all strings automatically get those changes.

NOTE *While it may be fun and interesting to modify built-in objects to experiment with functionality, it's not a good idea to do so in a production environment. Developers expect built-in objects to behave a certain way and have certain methods. Deliberately altering built-in objects violates those expectations and makes other developers unsure how the objects should work.*

Summary

Constructors are just normal functions that are called with the new operator. You can define your own constructors anytime you want to create multiple objects with the same properties. You can identify objects created from constructors using instanceof or by accessing their constructor property directly.

Every function has a prototype property that defines any properties shared by objects created with a particular constructor. Shared methods and primitive value properties are typically defined on prototypes, while all other properties are defined within the constructor. The constructor property is actually defined on the prototype because it is shared among object instances.

The prototype of an object is stored internally in the [[Prototype]] property. This property is a reference, not a copy. If you change the prototype at any point in time, those changes will occur on all instances because of the way JavaScript looks up properties. When you try to access a property on an object, that object is searched for any own property with the name you specify. If an own property is not found, the prototype is searched. This searching mechanism means the prototype can continue to change, and object instances referencing that prototype will reflect those changes immediately.

Built-in objects also have prototypes that can be modified. While it's not recommended to do this in production, it can be helpful for experimentation and proofs of concept for new functionality.

5

INHERITANCE

Learning how to create objects is the first step to understanding object-oriented programming. The second step is to understand inheritance. In traditional object-oriented languages, classes inherit properties from other classes. In JavaScript, however, inheritance can occur between objects with no classlike structure defining the relationship. The mechanism for this inheritance is one with which you are already familiar: prototypes.

Prototype Chaining and Object.prototype

JavaScript's built-in approach for inheritance is called *prototype chaining*, or *prototypal inheritance*. As you learned in Chapter 4, prototype properties are automatically available on object instances, which is a form of inheritance. The object instances inherit properties from the prototype. Because the prototype is also an object, it has its own prototype and inherits properties from that. This is the *prototype chain*: An object inherits from its prototype, while that prototype in turn inherits from its prototype, and so on.

All objects, including those you define yourself, automatically inherit from Object unless you specify otherwise (discussed later in this chapter). More specifically, all objects inherit from Object.prototype. Any object defined via an object literal has its [[Prototype]] set to Object.prototype, meaning that it inherits properties from Object.prototype, just like book in this example:

```
var book = {
    title: "The Principles of Object-Oriented JavaScript"
};

var prototype = Object.getPrototypeOf(book);

console.log(prototype === Object.prototype);        // true
```

Here, book has a prototype equal to Object.prototype. No additional code was necessary to make this happen, as this is the default behavior when new objects are created. This relationship means that book automatically receives methods from Object.prototype.

Methods Inherited from Object.prototype

Several of the methods used in the past couple of chapters are actually defined on Object.prototype and are therefore inherited by all other objects. Those methods are:

hasOwnProperty()   Determines whether an own property with the given name exists

propertyIsEnumerable()   Determines whether an own property is enumerable

isPrototypeOf()   Determines whether the object is the prototype of another

valueOf()   Returns the value representation of the object

toString()   Returns a string representation of the object

These five methods appear on all objects through inheritance. The last two are important when you need to make objects work consistently in JavaScript, and sometimes you might want to define them yourself.

valueOf()

The valueOf() method gets called whenever an operator is used on an object. By default, valueOf() simply returns the object instance. The primitive wrapper types override valueOf() so that it returns a string for String, a Boolean for Boolean, and a number for Number. Likewise, the Date object's valueOf() method returns the epoch time in milliseconds (just as Date.prototype.getTime() does). This is what allows you to write code that compares dates such as:

```
var now = new Date();
var earlier = new Date(2010, 1, 1);

console.log(now > earlier);          // true
```
❶

In this example, now is a Date representing the current time, and earlier is a fixed date in the past. When the greater-than operator (>) is used ❶, the valueOf() method is called on both objects before the comparison is performed. You can even subtract one date from another and get the difference in epoch time because of valueOf().

You can always define your own valueOf() method if your objects are intended to be used with operators. If you do define a valueOf() method, keep in mind that you're not changing how the operator works, only what value is used with the operator's default behavior.

toString()

The toString() method is called as a fallback whenever valueOf() returns a reference value instead of a primitive value. It is also implicitly called on primitive values whenever JavaScript is expecting a string. For example, when a string is used as one operand for the plus operator, the other operand is automatically converted to a string. If the other operand is a primitive value, it is converted into a string representation (for example, true becomes "true"), but if it is a reference value, then valueOf() is called. If valueOf() returns a reference value, toString() is called and the returned value is used. For example:

```
var book = {
    title: "The Principles of Object-Oriented JavaScript"
};

var message = "Book = " + book;
console.log(message);               // "Book = [object Object]"
```

This code constructs the string by combining "Book = " with book. Since book is an object, its toString() method is called. That method is inherited from Object.prototype and returns the default value of "[object Object]" in most JavaScript engines. If you are happy with that value, there's no need to change your object's toString() method. Sometimes, however, it's useful to define your own toString() method so that string conversions return a value that gives more information. Suppose, for example, that you want the previous script to log the book's title:

```
var book = {
    title: "The Principles of Object-Oriented JavaScript",
    toString: function() {
        return "[Book " + this.title + "]"
    }
};

var message = "Book = " + book;

// "Book = [Book The Principles of Object-Oriented JavaScript]"
❶ console.log(message);
```

This code defines a custom toString() method for book that returns a more useful value ❶ than the inherited version. You don't usually need to worry about defining a custom toString() method, but it's good to know that it's possible to do so if necessary.

Modifying Object.prototype

All objects inherit from Object.prototype by default, so changes to Object .prototype affect all objects. That's a very dangerous situation. You were advised in Chapter 4 not to modify built-in object prototypes, and that advice goes double for Object.prototype. Take a look at what can happen:

```
Object.prototype.add = function(value) {
    return this + value;
};

var book = {
    title: "The Principles of Object-Oriented JavaScript"
};

console.log(book.add(5));          // "[object Object]5"
console.log("title".add("end"));   // "titleend"

// in a web browser
console.log(document.add(true));   // "[object HTMLDocument]true"
console.log(window.add(5));        // "[object Window]true"
```

Adding `Object.prototype.add()` causes all objects to have an `add()` method, whether or not it actually makes sense. This problem has been an issue not just for developers but also for the committee that works on the JavaScript language: It has had to put new methods in different locations because adding methods to `Object.prototype` can have unforeseen consequences.

Another aspect of this problem involves adding enumerable properties to `Object.prototype`. In the previous example, `Object.prototype.add()` is an enumerable property, which means it will show up when you use a `for-in` loop, such as:

```
var empty = {};

for (var property in empty) {
    console.log(property);
}
```

Here, an empty object will still output "add" as a property because it exists on the prototype and is enumerable. Given how often the `for-in` construct is used in JavaScript, modifying `Object.prototype` with enumerable properties has the potential to affect a lot of code. For this reason, Douglas Crockford recommends using `hasOwnProperty()` in `for-in` loops all the time,* such as:

```
var empty = {};

for (var property in empty) {
    if (empty.hasOwnProperty(property)) {
        console.log(property);
    }
}
```

While this approach is effective against possible unwanted prototype properties, it also limits the use of `for-in` to only own properties, which may or may not be want you want. Your best bet for the most flexibility is to not modify `Object.prototype`.

Object Inheritance

The simplest type of inheritance is between objects. All you have to do is specify what object should be the new object's [[Prototype]]. Object literals have `Object.prototype` set as their [[Prototype]] implicitly, but you can also explicitly specify [[Prototype]] with the `Object.create()` method.

---

* See Douglas Crockford's "Code Conventions for the JavaScript Programming Language" (*http://javascript.crockford.com/code.html*).

The `Object.create()` method accepts two arguments. The first argument is the object to use for `[[Prototype]]` in the new object. The optional second argument is an object of property descriptors in the same format used by `Object.defineProperties()` (see Chapter 3). Consider the following:

```
var book = {
    title: "The Principles of Object-Oriented JavaScript"
};

// is the same as

var book = Object.create(Object.prototype, {
            title: {
                configurable: true,
                enumerable: true,
                value: "The Principles of Object-Oriented JavaScript",
                writable: true
            }
        });
```

The two declarations in this code are effectively the same. The first declaration uses an object literal to define an object with a single property called `title`. That object automatically inherits from `Object.prototype`, and the property is set to be configurable, enumerable, and writable by default. The second declaration takes the same steps but does so explicitly using `Object.create()`. The resulting `book` object from each declaration behaves the exact same way. But you'll probably never write code that inherits from `Object.prototype` directly, because you get that by default. Inheriting from other objects is much more interesting:

```
var person1 = {
    name: "Nicholas",
    sayName: function() {
        console.log(this.name);
    }
};

var person2 = Object.create(person1, {
    name: {
        configurable: true,
        enumerable: true,
        value: "Greg",
        writable: true
    }
});

person1.sayName();          // outputs "Nicholas"
person2.sayName();          // outputs "Greg"
```

```
console.log(person1.hasOwnProperty("sayName"));    // true
console.log(person1.isPrototypeOf(person2));       // true
console.log(person2.hasOwnProperty("sayName"));    // false
```

This code creates an object, person1, with a name property and a sayName()
method. The person2 object inherits from person1, so it inherits both name and
sayName(). However, person2 is defined via Object.create(), which also defines
an own name property for person2. This own property shadows the prototype
property of the same name and is used in its place. So, person1.sayName() outputs "Nicholas", while person2.sayName() outputs "Greg". Keep in mind that
sayName() still exists only on person1 and is being inherited by person2.

The inheritance chain in this example is longer for person2 than it is for
person1. The person2 object inherits from the person1 object, and the person1
object inherits from Object.prototype. See Figure 5-1.

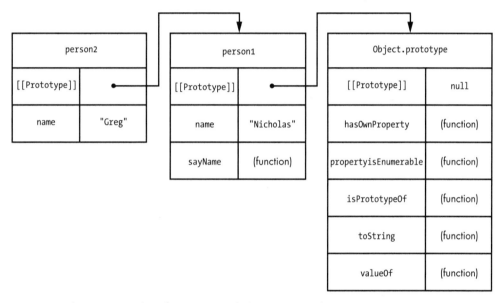

Figure 5-1: The prototype chain for person2 includes person1 and Object.prototype.

When a property is accessed on an object, the JavaScript engine goes
through a search process. If the property is found on the instance (that is,
if it's an own property), that property value is used. If the property is not
found on the instance, the search continues on [[Prototype]]. If the property
is still not found, the search continues to that object's [[Prototype]], and
so on until the end of the chain is reached. That chain usually ends with
Object.prototype, whose [[Prototype]] is set to null.

You can also create objects with a `null` `[[Prototype]]` via `Object.create()`, such as:

```
var nakedObject = Object.create(null);

console.log("toString" in nakedObject);    // false
console.log("valueOf" in nakedObject);     // false
```

The `nakedObject` in this example is an object with no prototype chain. That means built-in methods such as `toString()` and `valueOf()` aren't present on the object. In effect, this object is a completely blank slate with no predefined properties, which makes it perfect for creating a lookup hash without potential naming collisions with inherited property names. There aren't many other uses for an object like this, and you can't use it as if it were inheriting from `Object.prototype`. For example, any time you use an operator on `nakedObject`, you'll just get an error along the lines of "Cannot convert object to primitive value." Still, it's an interesting quirk of the JavaScript language that you can create a prototype-less object.

Constructor Inheritance

Object inheritance in JavaScript is also the basis of constructor inheritance. Recall from Chapter 4 that almost every function has a `prototype` property that can be modified or replaced. That `prototype` property is automatically assigned to be a new generic object that inherits from `Object.prototype` and has a single own property called `constructor`. In effect, the JavaScript engine does the following for you:

```
// you write this
function YourConstructor() {
    // initialization
}

// JavaScript engine does this for you behind the scenes
YourConstructor.prototype = Object.create(Object.prototype, {
                    constructor: {
                        configurable: true,
                        enumerable: true,
                        value: YourConstructor
                        writable: true
                    }
                });
```

So without doing anything extra, this code sets the constructor's prototype property to an object that inherits from `Object.prototype`, which means any instances of `YourConstructor` also inherit from `Object.prototype`. `YourConstructor` is a *subtype* of `Object`, and `Object` is a *supertype* of `YourConstructor`.

Because the prototype property is writable, you can change the proto-type chain by overwriting it. Consider the following example:

```
❶ function Rectangle(length, width) {
      this.length = length;
      this.width = width;
  }

  Rectangle.prototype.getArea = function() {
      return this.length * this.width;
  };

  Rectangle.prototype.toString = function() {
      return "[Rectangle " + this.length + "x" + this.width + "]";
  };

  // inherits from Rectangle
❷ function Square(size) {
      this.length = size;
      this.width = size;
  }

  Square.prototype = new Rectangle();
  Square.prototype.constructor = Square;

  Square.prototype.toString = function() {
      return "[Square " + this.length + "x" + this.width + "]";
  };

  var rect = new Rectangle(5, 10);
  var square = new Square(6);

  console.log(rect.getArea());        // 50
  console.log(square.getArea());      // 36

  console.log(rect.toString());       // "[Rectangle 5x10]"
  console.log(square.toString());     // "[Square 6x6]"

  console.log(rect instanceof Rectangle);    // true
  console.log(rect instanceof Object);       // true

  console.log(square instanceof Square);      // true
  console.log(square instanceof Rectangle);   // true
  console.log(square instanceof Object);      // true
```

In this code, there are two constructors: Rectangle ❶ and Square ❷. The Square constructor has its prototype property overwritten with an instance of Rectangle. No arguments are passed into Rectangle at this point because they don't need to be used, and if they were, all instances of Square would share the same dimensions. To change the prototype chain this way, you always need to make sure that the constructor won't throw an error if the arguments aren't supplied (many constructors contain initialization logic that may require the arguments) and that the constructor isn't altering any sort of global state, such as keeping track of how many instances have been created. The constructor property is restored on Square.prototype after the original value is overwritten.

After that, rect is created as an instance of Rectangle, and square is created as an instance of Square. Both objects have the getArea() method because it is inherited from Rectangle.prototype. The square variable is considered an instance of Square as well as Rectangle and Object because instanceof uses the prototype chain to determine the object type. See Figure 5-2.

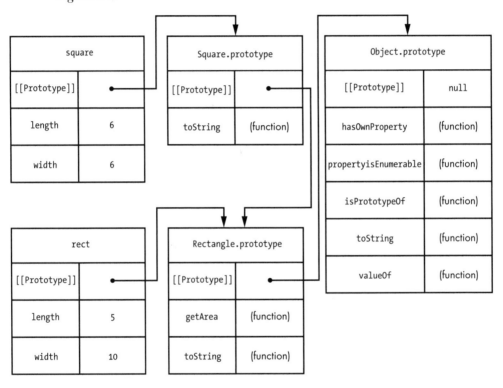

Figure 5-2: The prototype chains for square and rect show that both inherit from Rectangle.prototype and Object.prototype, but only square inherits from Square.prototype.

Square.prototype doesn't actually need to be overwritten with a Rectangle object, though; the Rectangle constructor isn't doing anything that is necessary for Square. In fact, the only relevant part is that Square.prototype needs to somehow link to Rectangle.prototype in order for inheritance to happen. That means you can simplify this example by using Object.create() once again.

```
// inherits from Rectangle
function Square(size) {
    this.length = size;
    this.width = size;
}

Square.prototype = Object.create(Rectangle.prototype, {
                        constructor: {
                            configurable: true,
                            enumerable: true,
                            value: Square,
                            writable: true
                        }
                    });

Square.prototype.toString = function() {
    return "[Square " + this.length + "x" + this.width + "]";
};
```

In this version of the code, `Square.prototype` is overwritten with a
new object that inherits from `Rectangle.prototype`, and the `Rectangle`
constructor is never called. That means you don't need to worry about
causing an error by calling the constructor without arguments anymore.
Otherwise, this code behaves exactly the same as the previous code. The
prototype chain remains intact, so all instances of `Square` inherit from
`Rectangle.prototype` and the constructor is restored in the same step.

NOTE   *Always make sure that you overwrite the prototype* before *adding properties to it,
or you will lose the added methods when the overwrite happens.*

Constructor Stealing

Because inheritance is accomplished through prototype chains in
JavaScript, you don't need to call an object's supertype constructor. If
you do want to call the supertype constructor from the subtype constructor, then you need to take advantage of how JavaScript functions work.
   In Chapter 2, you learned about the `call()` and `apply()` methods,
which allow functions to be called with a different this value. That's
exactly how *constructor stealing* works. You simply call the supertype constructor from the subtype constructor using either `call()` or `apply()` to
pass in the newly created object. In effect, you're stealing the supertype
constructor for your own object, as in this example:

```
function Rectangle(length, width) {
    this.length = length;
    this.width = width;
}
```

```
    Rectangle.prototype.getArea = function() {
        return this.length * this.width;
    };

    Rectangle.prototype.toString = function() {
        return "[Rectangle " + this.length + "x" + this.width + "]";
    };

    // inherits from Rectangle
❶  function Square(size) {
        Rectangle.call(this, size, size);

        // optional: add new properties or override existing ones here
    }

    Square.prototype = Object.create(Rectangle.prototype, {
                            constructor: {
                                configurable: true,
                                enumerable: true,
                                value: Square,
                                writable: true
                            }
                        });

    Square.prototype.toString = function() {
        return "[Square " + this.length + "x" + this.width + "]";
    };

    var square = new Square(6);

    console.log(square.length);        // 6
    console.log(square.width);         // 6
    console.log(square.getArea());     // 36
```

The ❶ Square constructor calls the Rectangle constructor and passes in
this as well as size two times (once for length and once for width). Doing
so creates the length and width properties on the new object and makes
each equal to size. This is the way to avoid redefining properties from a
constructor from which you want to inherit. You can add new properties
or override existing ones after applying the super type constructor.

This two-step process is useful when you need to accomplish inheritance between custom types. You'll always need to modify a constructor's
prototype, and you may also need to call the supertype constructor from
within the subtype constructor. Generally, you'll modify the prototype
for method inheritance and use constructor stealing for properties. This
approach is typically referred to as *pseudoclassical inheritance* because it
mimics classical inheritance from class-based languages.

Accessing Supertype Methods

In the previous example, the Square type has its own toString() method that shadows toString() on the prototype. It is fairly common to override supertype methods with new functionality in the subtype, but what if you still want to access the supertype method? In other languages, you might be able to say super.toString(), but JavaScript doesn't have anything similar. Instead, you can directly access the method on the supertype's prototype and use either call() or apply() to execute the method on the subtype object. For example:

```
function Rectangle(length, width) {
    this.length = length;
    this.width = width;
}

Rectangle.prototype.getArea = function() {
    return this.length * this.width;
};

Rectangle.prototype.toString = function() {
    return "[Rectangle " + this.length + "x" + this.height + "]";
};

// inherits from Rectangle
function Square(size) {
    Rectangle.call(this, size, size);
}

Square.prototype = Object.create(Rectangle.prototype, {
                        constructor: {
                            configurable: true,
                            enumerable: true,
                            value: Square,
                            writable: true
                        }
                });

// call the supertype method
❶ Square.prototype.toString = function() {
    var text = Rectangle.prototype.toString.call(this);
    return text.replace("Rectangle", "Square");
};
```

In this version of the code, ❶ Square.prototype.toString() calls Rectangle.prototype.toString() by using call(). The method just needs to replace "Rectangle" with "Square" before returning the resulting text. This approach may seem a bit verbose for such a simple operation, but it is the only way to access a supertype's method.

Summary

JavaScript supports inheritance through prototype chaining. A prototype chain is created between objects when the [[Prototype]] of one object is set equal to another. All generic objects automatically inherit from Object .prototype. If you want to create an object that inherits from something else, you can use Object.create() to specify the value of [[Prototype]] for a new object.

You accomplish inheritance between custom types by creating a prototype chain on the constructor. By setting the constructor's prototype property to another value, you create inheritance between instances of the custom type and the prototype of that other value. All instances of that constructor share the same prototype, so they all inherit from the same object. This technique works very well for inheriting methods from other objects, but you cannot inherit own properties using prototypes.

To inherit own properties correctly, you can use constructor stealing, which is simply calling a constructor function using call() or apply() so that any initialization is done on the subtype object. Combining constructor stealing and prototype chaining is the most common way to achieve inheritance between custom types in JavaScript. This combination is frequently called pseudoclassical inheritance because of its similarity to inheritance in class-based languages.

You can access methods on a supertype by directly accessing the supertype's prototype. In doing so, you must use call() or apply() to execute the supertype method on the subtype object.

6

OBJECT PATTERNS

JavaScript has many patterns for creating objects, and there's usually more than one way to accomplish the same thing. You can define your own custom types or your own generic objects whenever you want. You can use inheritance to share behavior between objects, or you can employ other techniques, such as mixins. You can also take advantage of advanced JavaScript features to prevent an object's structure from being modified. The patterns discussed in this chapter give you powerful ways of managing and creating objects, all based on your use cases.

Private and Privileged Members

All object properties in JavaScript are public, and there's no explicit way to indicate that a property shouldn't be accessed from outside a particular object. At some point, however, you might not want data to be public. For example, when an object uses a value to determine some sort of state, modifying that data without the object's knowledge throws the state management process into chaos. One way to avoid this is by using naming conventions. For example, it's quite common to prefix properties with an underscore (such as this._name) when they are not intended to be public. However, there are ways of hiding data that don't rely on convention and are therefore more "bulletproof" in preventing the modification of private information.

The Module Pattern

The *module pattern* is an object-creation pattern designed to create singleton objects with private data. The basic approach is to use an *immediately invoked function expression (IIFE)* that returns an object. An IIFE is a function expression that is defined and then called immediately to produce a result. That function expression can contain any number of local variables that aren't accessible from outside that function. Because the returned object is defined within that function, the object's methods have access to the data. (All objects defined within the IIFE have access to the same local variables.) Methods that access private data in this way are called *privileged* methods. Here's the basic format for the module pattern:

```
var yourObject = (function() {

    // private data variables

    return {
        // public methods and properties
    };

❶ }());
```

In this pattern, an anonymous function is created and executed immediately. (Note the extra parentheses at the end of the function ❶. You can execute anonymous functions immediately using this syntax.) That means the function exists for just a moment, is executed, and then is destroyed. IIFEs are a very popular pattern in JavaScript, partially for their use in the module pattern.

The module pattern allows you to use regular variables as de facto object properties that aren't exposed publicly. You accomplish this by creating *closure* functions as object methods. Closures are simply functions that access data outside their own scope. For example, whenever you access a global object in a function, such as window in a web browser, that function is accessing a variable outside its own scope. The difference with the module function is that the variables are declared within the IIFE, and a function that is also declared inside the IIFE accesses those variables. For example:

```
var person = (function() {

❶    var age = 25;

    return {
        name: "Nicholas",

❷        getAge: function() {
            return age;
        },

❸        growOlder: function() {
            age++;
        }
    };

}());

console.log(person.name);       // "Nicholas"
console.log(person.getAge());   // 25

person.age = 100;
console.log(person.getAge());   // 25

person.growOlder();
console.log(person.getAge());   // 26
```

This code creates the person object using the module pattern. The age variable ❶ acts like a private property for the object. It can't be accessed directly from outside the object, but it can be used by the object methods. There are two privileged methods on the object: getAge() ❷, which reads the value of the age variable, and growOlder() ❸, which increments age. Both of these methods can access the variable age directly because it is defined in the outer function in which they are defined.

There is a variation of the module pattern called the *revealing module pattern*, which arranges all variables and methods at the top of the IIFE and simply assigns them to the returned object. You can write the previous example using the revealing module pattern as follows:

```
var person = (function() {

    var age = 25;

    function getAge() {
        return age;
    }

    function growOlder() {
        age++;
    }

    return {
        name: "Nicholas",
❶       getAge: getAge,
        growOlder: growOlder
    };

}());
```

In the revealing module pattern, age, getAge(), and growOlder() are all defined as local to the IIFE. The getAge() and growOlder() functions are then assigned to the returned object ❶, effectively "revealing" them outside the IIFE. This code is essentially the same as the earlier example using the traditional module pattern; however, some prefer this pattern because it keeps all variable and function declarations together.

Private Members for Constructors

The module pattern is great for defining individual objects that have private properties, but what about custom types that also require their own private properties? You can use a pattern that's similar to the module pattern inside the constructor to create instance-specific private data. For example:

```
function Person(name) {

    // define a variable only accessible inside of the Person constructor
    var age = 25;

    this.name = name;

❶   this.getAge = function() {
        return age;
    };
```

```
❷      this.growOlder = function() {
           age++;
       };
   }

   var person = new Person("Nicholas");

   console.log(person.name);        // "Nicholas"
   console.log(person.getAge());    // 25

   person.age = 100;
   console.log(person.getAge());    // 25

   person.growOlder();
   console.log(person.getAge());    // 26
```

In this code, the Person constructor has a local variable, age. That variable is used as part of the getAge() ❶ and growOlder() ❷ methods. When you create an instance of Person, that instance receives its own age variable, getAge() method, and growOlder() method. In many ways, this is similar to the module pattern, where the constructor creates a local scope and returns the this object. As discussed in Chapter 4, placing methods on an object instance is less efficient than doing so on the prototype, but this is the only approach possible when you want private, instance-specific data.

If you want private data to be shared across all instances (as if it were on the prototype), you can use a hybrid approach that looks like the module pattern but uses a constructor:

```
   var Person = (function() {

       // everyone shares the same age
❶      var age = 25;

❷      function InnerPerson(name) {
           this.name = name;
       }

       InnerPerson.prototype.getAge = function() {
           return age;
       };

       InnerPerson.prototype.growOlder = function() {
           age++;
       };

       return InnerPerson;

   }());
```

```
var person1 = new Person("Nicholas");
var person2 = new Person("Greg");

console.log(person1.name);        // "Nicholas"
console.log(person1.getAge());    // 25

console.log(person2.name);        // "Greg"
console.log(person2.getAge());    // 25

person1.growOlder();
console.log(person1.getAge());    // 26
console.log(person2.getAge());    // 26
```

In this code, the InnerPerson constructor ❷ is defined inside an IIFE.
The variable age ❶ is defined outside the constructor but is used for
two prototype methods. The InnerPerson constructor is then returned
and becomes the Person constructor in the global scope. All instances of
Person end up sharing the age variable, so changing the value with one
instance automatically affects the other instance.

Mixins

Although pseudoclassical inheritance and prototypal inheritance are
used frequently in JavaScript, there is also a type of pseudoinheritance
accomplished through mixins. *Mixins* occur when one object acquires the
properties of another without modifying the prototype chain. The first
object (a *receiver*) actually receives the properties of the second object (the
supplier) by copying those properties directly. Traditionally, you create
mixins using a function such as this:

```
function mixin(receiver, supplier) {
    for (var property in supplier) {
        if (supplier.hasOwnProperty(property)) {
            receiver[property] = supplier[property]
        }
    }

    return receiver;
}
```

The mixin() function accepts two arguments: the receiver and the supplier. The goal of the function is to copy all enumerable properties from
the supplier onto the receiver. You accomplish this using a for-in loop
that iterates over the properties in supplier and then assigns the value

of that property to a property of the same name on receiver. Keep in mind that this is a shallow copy, so if a property contains an object, then both the supplier and the receiver will be pointing to the same object. This pattern is used frequently for adding new behaviors to JavaScript objects that already exist on other objects.

For example, you can add event support to an object through a mixin rather than inheritance. First, suppose you've already defined a custom type for using events:

```
function EventTarget(){
}

EventTarget.prototype = {

    constructor: EventTarget,

❶    addListener: function(type, listener){

        // create an array if it doesn't exist
        if (!this.hasOwnProperty("_listeners")) {
            this._listeners = [];
        }

        if (typeof this._listeners[type] == "undefined"){
            this._listeners[type] = [];
        }

        this._listeners[type].push(listener);
    },

❷    fire: function(event){

        if (!event.target){
            event.target = this;
        }

        if (!event.type){  // falsy
            throw new Error("Event object missing 'type' property.");
        }

        if (this._listeners && this._listeners[event.type] instanceof Array){
            var listeners = this._listeners[event.type];
            for (var i=0, len=listeners.length; i < len; i++){
                listeners[i].call(this, event);
            }
        }
    },
```

```
❸    removeListener: function(type, listener){
        if (this._listeners && this._listeners[type] instanceof Array){
            var listeners = this._listeners[type];
            for (var i=0, len=listeners.length; i < len; i++){
                if (listeners[i] === listener){
                    listeners.splice(i, 1);
                    break;
                }
            }
        }
    }
};
```

The EventTarget type provides basic event handling for any object. You can add ❶ and remove ❸ listeners as well as fire events ❷ directly on the object. The event listeners are stored on a _listeners property that is created only when addListener() is called for the first time (this makes it easier to mix in). You can use instances of EventTarget like this:

```
var target = new EventTarget();
target.addListener("message", function(event) {
    console.log("Message is " + event.data);
})

target.fire({
    type: "message",
    data: "Hello world!"
});
```

Support for events is useful for objects in JavaScript. If you want to have a different type of object that also supports events, you have a few options. First, you can create a new instance of EventTarget and then add on the properties that you want:

```
var person = new EventTarget();
person.name = "Nicholas";
person.sayName = function() {
    console.log(this.name);
    this.fire({ type: "namesaid", name: name });
};
```

In this code, a new variable called person is created as an instance of EventTarget, and then the person-related properties are added. Unfortunately, this means that person is actually an instance of EventTarget instead of Object or a custom type. You also incur the overhead of needing to add a bunch of new properties by hand. It would be better to have a more organized way of doing this.

A second way to solve this problem is to use pseudoclassical inheritance:

```
function Person(name) {
    this.name = name;
}

Person.prototype = Object.create(EventTarget.prototype);
Person.prototype.constructor = Person;

Person.prototype.sayName = function() {
    console.log(this.name);
    this.fire({ type: "namesaid", name: name });
};

var person = new Person("Nicholas");

console.log(person instanceof Person);      // true
console.log(person instanceof EventTarget); // true
```

In this case, there is a new Person type that inherits from EventTarget ❶. You can add any further methods you need to Person's prototype afterward. However, this isn't as succinct as it could be, and you could argue that the relationship doesn't make sense: A person is a type of event target? By using a mixin instead, you can reduce the amount of code necessary to assign those new properties to the prototype:

```
function Person(name) {
    this.name = name;
}

mixin(Person.prototype, new EventTarget());
mixin(Person.prototype, {
    constructor: Person,

    sayName: function() {
        console.log(this.name);
        this.fire({ type: "namesaid", name: name });
    }
});

var person = new Person("Nicholas");

console.log(person instanceof Person);      // true
console.log(person instanceof EventTarget); // false
```

Here, Person.prototype is mixed in with a new instance of EventTarget ❶ to get the event behavior. Then, Person.prototype is mixed in with constructor and sayName() to complete the composition of the prototype. Instances of Person are not instances of EventTarget in this example because there is no inheritance.

Of course, you might decide that while you do want to use an object's properties, you don't want a constructor of pseudoclassical inheritance at all. In that case, you can use a mixin directly when you create your new object:

```
var person = mixin(new EventTarget(), {

    name: "Nicholas",

    sayName: function() {
        console.log(this.name);
        this.fire({ type: "namesaid", name: name });
    }

});
```

In this example, a new instance of `EventTarget` is mixed in with some new properties to create the `person` object without affecting person's prototype chain.

One thing to keep in mind about using mixins in this way is that accessor properties on the supplier become data properties on the receiver, which means you can overwrite them if you're not careful. That's because the receiver properties are being created by assignment rather than by `Object.defineProperty()`, meaning the current value of the supplier property is read and then assigned to a property of the same name on the receiver. For example:

```
var person = mixin(new EventTarget(), {

❶    get name() {
        return "Nicholas"
    },

    sayName: function() {
        console.log(this.name);
        this.fire({ type: "namesaid", name: name });
    }

});

console.log(person.name);        // "Nicholas"

❷ person.name = "Greg";
console.log(person.name);        // "Greg"
```

In this code, name is defined as an accessor property with only a getter ❶. That means assigning a value to the property should have no effect. However, because the accessor property becomes a data property on the person object, it's possible to overwrite name with a new value ❷. During the call to mixin(), the value of name is read from the supplier and assigned to the property called name on the receiver. At no point during this process is a new accessor defined, making the name property on the receiver a data property.

If you want accessor properties to be copied over as accessor properties, you need a different mixin() function, such as:

```
function mixin(receiver, supplier) {
❶    Object.keys(supplier).forEach(function(property) {
         var descriptor = Object.getOwnPropertyDescriptor(supplier, property);
❷        Object.defineProperty(receiver, property, descriptor);
    });

    return receiver;
}

var person = mixin(new EventTarget(), {

    get name() {
        return "Nicholas"
    },

    sayName: function() {
        console.log(this.name);
        this.fire({ type: "namesaid", name: name });
    }

});

console.log(person.name);        // "Nicholas"

person.name = "Greg";
console.log(person.name);        // "Nicholas"
```

This version of mixin() uses Object.keys() ❶ to get an array of all enumerable own properties on supplier. The forEach() method is used to iterate over those properties. The property descriptor for each property on supplier is retrieved and then added to receiver via Object.defineProperty() ❷. This ensures that all of the relevant property information is transferred to receiver, not just the value. That means the person object has an accessor property called name, so it cannot be overwritten.

Of course, this version of mixin() works only in ECMAScript 5 JavaScript engines. If your code needs to work for older engines, you should combine the two mixin() approaches into a single function:

```
function mixin(receiver, supplier) {

❶    if (Object.getOwnPropertyDescriptor) {

        Object.keys(supplier).forEach(function(property) {
            var descriptor = Object.getOwnPropertyDescriptor(supplier, property);
            Object.defineProperty(receiver, property, descriptor);
        });

    } else {

❷        for (var property in supplier) {
            if (supplier.hasOwnProperty(property)) {
                receiver[property] = supplier[property]
            }
        }
    }

    return receiver;
}
```

Here, mixin() checks whether Object.getOwnPropertyDescriptor() ❶ exists to determine whether the JavaScript engine supports ECMAScript 5. If so, it goes on to use the ECMAScript 5 version. Otherwise, the ECMAScript 3 version is used ❷. This function is safe to use in both modern and legacy JavaScript engines, as they will apply the most appropriate mixin strategy.

NOTE *Keep in mind that Object.keys() returns only enumerable properties. If you want to also copy over nonenumerable properties, use Object.getOwnPropertyNames() instead.*

Scope-Safe Constructors

Because all constructors are just functions, you can call them without using the new operator and therefore affect the value of this. Doing so can yield unexpected results, as this ends up coerced to the global object in nonstrict mode, or the constructor throws an error in strict mode. In Chapter 4, you encountered this example:

```
function Person(name) {
    this.name = name;
}
```

```
Person.prototype.sayName = function() {
    console.log(this.name);
};
```

❶ `var person1 = Person("Nicholas");`   `// note: missing "new"`

```
console.log(person1 instanceof Person);    // false
console.log(typeof person1);               // "undefined"
console.log(name);                         // "Nicholas"
```

In this case, name is created as a global variable because the Person constructor is called without new ❶. Keep in mind that this code is running in nonstrict mode, as leaving out new would throw an error in strict mode. The fact that the constructor begins with a capital letter usually indicates that it should be preceded by new, but what if you want to allow this use case and have the function work without new? Many built-in constructors, such as Array and RegExp, also work without new because they are written to be *scope safe*. A scope-safe constructor can be called with or without new and returns the same type of object in either case.

When new is called with a function, the newly created object represented by this is already an instance of the custom type represented by the constructor. So you can use instanceof to determine whether new was used in the function call:

```
function Person(name) {
    if (this instanceof Person) {
        // called with "new"
    } else {
        // called without "new"
    }
}
```

Using a pattern like this lets you control what a function does based on whether it's called with new or without. You may want to treat each circumstance differently, but you'll often want the function to behave the same way (frequently, to protect against accidental omission of new). A scope-safe version of Person looks like this:

```
function Person(name) {
    if (this instanceof Person) {
        this.name = name;
    } else {
        return new Person(name);
    }
}
```

For this constructor, the `name` property is assigned as always when `new` is used. If `new` isn't used, the constructor is called recursively via `new` to create a proper instance of the object. In this way, the following are equivalent:

```
var person1 = new Person("Nicholas");
var person2 = Person("Nicholas");

console.log(person1 instanceof Person);    // true
console.log(person2 instanceof Person);    // true
```

Creating new objects without using the `new` operator is becoming more common as an effort to curb errors caused by omitting `new`. JavaScript itself has several reference types with scope-safe constructors, such as `Object`, `Array`, `RegExp`, and `Error`.

Summary

There are many different ways to create and compose objects in JavaScript. While JavaScript does not include the formal concept of private properties, you can create data or functions that are accessible only from within an object. For singleton objects, you can use the module pattern to hide data from the outside world. You can use an immediately invoked function expression (IIFE) to define local variables and functions that are accessible only by the newly created object. Privileged methods are methods on the object that have access to private data. You can also create constructors that have private data by either defining variables in the constructor function or by using an IIFE to create private data that is shared among all instances.

Mixins are a powerful way to add functionality to objects while avoiding inheritance. A mixin copies properties from one object to another so that the receiving object gains functionality without inheriting from the supplying object. Unlike inheritance, mixins do not allow you to identify where the capabilities came from after the object is created. For this reason, mixins are best used with data properties or small pieces of functionality. Inheritance is still preferable when you want to obtain more functionality and know where that functionality came from.

Scope-safe constructors are constructors that you can call with or without `new` to create a new object instance. This pattern takes advantage of the fact that `this` is an instance of the custom type as soon as the constructor begins to execute, which lets you alter the constructor's behavior depending on whether or not you used the `new` operator.

INDEX

in operator, 53
    testing for property instance
        with, 33–34
instanceof operator, 12–13
    temporary objects and, 15
instances. *See also* objects
    checking type of, 50–51
    prototype link to constructor, 60
    of reference types, 6
instantiating
    built-in types, 8–11
    objects, 6
    primitive wrappers, 16
internal property, of functions, 17
isArray() method, 13–14
isExtensible() method, 45, 46
isFrozen() method, 47
isPrototypeOf() method, 55, 66
isSealed() method, 46

K

keys() method, 36, 89–90
key/value pairs, 48

L

length property, of functions, 21–22
literals, 3, 9
    array, 10
    function, 10–11
    object, 9–10
    regular expression, 11

M

memory location, pointer to, 7
methods, 6, 24–28
    adding to arrays, 62
    primitive, 6
    privileged, 80
    prototypes for defining, 57–60
    for supertypes, accessing, 77
mixins, 84–90
    data properties from, 88–89
module patterns, 80–82

N

names
    for constructors,
        capitalization of, 50
    multiple functions with same, 23
    for properties, 80

new operator, 6, 90–92
    constructors and, 49, 50, 52
    instantiating reference types with, 9
    this object created with, 51
null value, 3
    determining if a value is, 5
    setting object variable to, 7–8
    setting property to, 35
    typeof operator and, 5
Number primitive wrapper type, 14–15
number type, 3

O

Object built-in type, 9
Object constructor, 32
Object.create() method, 70
Object.defineProperties() method, 43–44
Object.defineProperty() method,
        39–41, 52
Object.freeze() method, 47, 61
Object.getOwnPropertyDescriptor()
        method, 44
Object.getPrototypeOf() method, 55
Object.isExtensible() method, 45, 46
Object.isFrozen() method, 47
Object.isSealed() method, 46
Object.keys() method, 36, 89–90
object literals, 9–10
object patterns, 79–92
    private and privileged
        members, 80–84
Object.preventExtensions() method, 45
Object.prototype.isPrototypeOf() method,
        55, 66
Object.prototype prototype
    methods inherited from, 66–68
    modifying, 68–69
objects, 2, 6, 31–48
    creating, 6–7
    dereferencing, 7–8
    freezing, 47
    inheritance, 69–72
    methods, 24–28
    modification, preventing, 45–47
    properties, defining, 32–33
    property inheritance from
        prototype, 65–69
    reference types as, 2
    sealing, 45–46
Object.seal() method, 45–46, 61
overloading functions, 23–24

own properties
    determining existence of, 66
    determining whether
        enumerable, 66
    in operator to check for, 34
    for objects, 32
    vs. prototype properties, 55–56

P

parameters, 21–22
person object, module pattern for
        creating, 81
pointer to memory location, 7
preventExtensions() method, 45
preventing object modifications, 45–47
primitive methods, 6
primitive types, 2, 3–6
primitive wrapper types, 14–16
private data, sharing, 83–84
private members, 80–84
    for constructors, 82–84
privileged members, 80–84
properties, 6, 11–12, 80
    adding or removing, 8
    copying enumerable, between
        receiver and supplier, 84–86
    creating on temporary objects, 15
    defining, 32–33
    defining multiple, 43–44
    detecting, 33–35
    enumerable, adding to
        Object.prototype, 69
    enumeration, 36–37
    identifying on prototype, 54
    removing, 35
    string literals for names, 9
    types, 37–38
property attributes, 38–44
    changing, 39–40
    retrieving, 44
propertyIsEnumerable() method, 37, 39, 66
proto property, 55
prototype chaining, 65–69, 71, 74
    object without, 72
    overwriting, 73
prototype properties
    identifying, 54
    vs. own properties, 55–56
prototype property, of functions, 53, 72
[[Prototype]] property, 54–56, 60–61

prototypes, 53–63
    built-in object, 62–63
    changing, 60–62
    identifying properties, 54
    overwriting, 59
    property inheritance from, 65–69
    use with constructors, 57–60
pseudoclassical inheritance, 76, 87
pseudoinheritance, mixins for, 84
[[Put]] method, 32–33
    for data properties, 37

R

read-only property, 38
receiver, copying enumerable
        properties between
        supplier and, 84–86
Rectangle constructor, 73–75
reference types, 2, 6–8
    identifying, 12–13
reference values, storing on prototype,
        57–58
RegExp built-in type, 9
RegExp constructor, 11
regular expression literals, 11
removing properties, 8, 35
retrieving property attributes, 44
revealing module pattern, 82

S

scope-safe constructors, 90–92
sealed objects, prototype modification
        and, 61
sealing objects, 45–46
seal() method, 45–46, 61
[[Set]] attribute, 32–33, 41
setter functions, 37–38
sharing private data, 83–84
signatures, function with multiple, 23
sort() method, 20
square brackets ([ ])
    for array literals, 10
    for property access, 11–12
Square constructor, 73–75
stealing constructors, 75–76
strict mode
    for nonextensible objects, 45
    for sealed objects, 46
string literals, as property names, 9
String primitive wrapper type, 14–15

strings
    capitalize() method, 62
    conversion of values to,
        for comparison, 21
    methods, 6
string type, 3
substring() method, 6
subtype constructors, 72, 75–76
sum() function, 21
supertype
    constructors, 72, 75–76
    methods, accessing, 77
supplier, copying enumerable
        properties between
        receiver and, 84–86

T

temporary objects, creating
        properties on, 15
this object, 25–26
    changing value of, 26–28
    to create length and width
        properties, 76
    creating with new, 51
toFixed() method, 6
toLowerCase() method, 6
toString() method, 6, 35, 66, 67–68
triple equals operator (===), 5
truthy values, 33
typeof operator, 4–5, 12
types, 2. *See also* primitive types;
        reference types
    checking for different, 24
    checking instance for, 50–51
    instantiating built-in, 8–11

U

undefined type, 3
underscore (_), in property name
        prefix, 38, 80

V

[[Value]] attribute, 40
valueOf() method, 66, 67
values
    functions as, 19–21
    passing, between web page
        frames, 13
variable object, 2
variables, for primitive types, 3–4

W

web pages, passing values between
        frames, 13
wrapper types, primitive, 14–16
[[Writable]] attribute, 40
write-only properties, 38

The Principles of Object-Oriented JavaScript is set in New Baskerville, Futura, TheSansMono Condensed, and Dogma. The book was printed and bound by Lake Book Manufacturing in Melrose Park, Illinois. The paper is 60# Husky Opaque Offset Smooth, which is certified by the Sustainable Forestry Initiative (SFI).

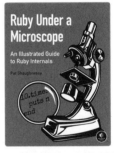